LOCAL ECONOMIC
DEVELOPMENT POLICY

CONTEMPORARY URBAN AFFAIRS
VOLUME I
GARLAND REFERENCE LIBRARY OF SOCIAL SCIENCE
VOLUME 1109

CONTEMPORARY URBAN AFFAIRS
RICHARD D. BINGHAM, *Series Editor*

LOCAL ECONOMIC
DEVELOPMENT POLICY
The United States and Canada
by Laura A. Reese

LOCAL ECONOMIC DEVELOPMENT POLICY
THE UNITED STATES AND CANADA

LAURA A. REESE

The Maxine
Goodman Levin
College of
Urban Affairs at
Cleveland State
University

THE
URBAN

CENTER

GARLAND PUBLISHING, INC.
NEW YORK AND LONDON
1997

Library of Congress Cataloging-in-Publication Data

Reese, Laura A., 1958–
    Local economic development policy : the United States and Canada / by
Laura A. Reese.
        p.   cm. — (Garland reference library of social science ; vol. 1109.
Contemporary urban affairs ; vol. 1)
    Includes bibliographical references and index.
    ISBN 0-8153-2383-2 (alk. paper)
    1. Economic development projects—United States.   2. Community de-
velopment—United States.   3. Bureaucracy—United States.   4. Economic
development projects—Canada.   5. Community development—Canada.
6. Bureaucracy—Canada.   I. Title. II. Series: Garland reference library of
social science ; v. 1109. III. Series: Garland reference library of social
science. Contemporary urban affairs ; vol. 1.
HC110.E44R44   1997
338.973—dc21   96–47040
                                                            CIP

Printed on acid-free, 250-year-life paper
Manufactured in the United States of America

To My Parents:

The late John E. and Janet B. Reese

CONTENTS

ACKNOWLEDGMENTS

This book culminates a number of years of work on local economic development policies and policy-making in the U.S. and Canada. Hence, there are many who have contributed to the project in substantial ways. Most importantly, I'd like to thank Professor Joseph Ohren for incalculable assistance and support in helping to conceive of the project, and reading, editing, and commenting on numerous drafts. More critically, since he is my husband as well as a colleague, I'd like to thank him for putting up with the project (and me) for the duration. Thanks are due to several friends and graduate assistants for graphics assistance: Lora Crombez, Lisa Shupra, and particularly Colleen Croxall. Professor David Fasenfest provided much needed and appreciated statistical and conceptual assistance. Parts of the research for this book have been supported by the Canadian Embassy Research Grant Program, Eastern Michigan University, and Wayne State University. Finally, I'd like to express thanks to Richard Bingham for supporting the project and reading several drafts and to David Estrin and Garland Publishing for helping it all come together.

SERIES EDITOR'S PREFACE

Laura Reese's *Local Economic Development Policy: The United States and Canada* launches the Contemporary Urban Affairs series by Garland Publishing. The series examines the changing face of urban areas: political, racial, economic, and physical. Subjects in the series include urban redevelopment, comparative urban studies, economic pressures and opportunities, suburban development, urban politics, racial/ethnic issues, and urban policy issues such as transportation, education, infrastructure, economic development, and intergovernmental relations.

Local Economic Development Policy: The United States and Canada provides an auspicious beginning for the new series. Laura Reese compares and analyzes local economic development efforts in Michigan and Ontario. She seeks to redress the paucity of literature comparing local economic development in the United States and Canada. Her goal is to "examine and refine current theories of economic development policy-making to include the role of professional bureaucrats and to test an explanatory model which operates cross-nationally."

Her study documents significant statutory differences of local economic development policies between the United States and Canada. At the same time, it shows that the similarities are greater than the differences. It is in the bureaucratic world where the differences really narrow. Economic development directors in both countries operate in the same basic environments, under the same general constraints, and generally in similar manners. Thus, from a theoretical perspective, Reese's cross-national research has increased our ability to generalize about urban economic development activities.

Richard D. Bingham

Local Economic Development Policy

CHAPTER 1

LOCAL ECONOMIC DEVELOPMENT POLICY IN A CROSS-NATIONAL CONTEXT

Among conversations with economic development officials, conference panels, research papers, and academic studies, two incidents stand out. One was a conversation with a local economic development practitioner. She was lamenting the often uncomfortable fit between her academic preparation and the realities of economic development policy-making and implementation. In an optimal world, she said, she would present elected officials and community leaders with policy recommendations based on rational planning, market studies, and cost benefit analyses, and the output of her work would be judged accordingly. However, after some time on the job, she commented: "Don't ask me about new jobs created, firm start-ups, or tax base growth resulting from economic development efforts . . . just ask me how many business leaders I've talked to today."

The second incident involved a practitioner presentation on a conference panel focusing on successful local economic development efforts--"model communities" if you will. One economic development director was describing the successful efforts of his community as ideal for emulation by others; "economic development in our community is like throwing spaghetti at the wall to see if it is properly cooked--we try everything and anything and eventually something will stick."

Mier and Bingham (1993) point to the value of such "metaphors" in helping scholars, students, and practitioners communicate and understand consistencies across disciplines and localities. These incidents serve as metaphors, providing important lessons about local economic development policy-making, which frame the theme of this book. First, while the rhetoric and ideal of rational planning abounds, the practice of economic development strays far from the mark in many cases. Second, this is not necessarily the result of a lack of knowledge on the part of practitioners. They appear to be fully aware of the ideals of rational planning; however, the exigencies of everyday life and local policy-making get in the way. Third, while elected officials and business leaders clearly have major roles in economic development, one cannot overlook the importance of economic development professionals and their impact on policy-making.

"CITY LIMITS" AND LOCAL OFFICIALS

For these lessons to have any currency it must first be concluded that local governments and officials can, in fact, affect their environment. This matter has been the subject of considerable debate in recent years. One argument emphasizes the external constraints on cities, suggesting that public officials basically react to external pressures (for example, Katznelson, 1976; Peterson, 1981; Molotch and Logan, 1985; Kantor, 1987). Such external forces include federal and state governmental policies, business location and production decisions, capital and labor flows, and even actions of other local governments. Assuming a common goal of expanded economic growth, economic development decision-makers will presumably "shoot anything that flies; claim anything that falls" (Rubin, 1988). Or, as in the comment earlier, throw spaghetti at the wall. In an effort to respond to local economic interests, local governments pursue expansionary policies in a "growth machine" process (Molotch and Logan, 1985). This dynamic produces a policy system where cities attempt all techniques with which they are familiar or which have been employed by their competition in an effort to obtain and retain the vaunted economic progress (Bingham, 1976; Bowman, 1988; Pelissero and Fasenfest, 1989).

An alternative view stresses the importance of local initiatives, essentially arguing that "politics does matter" and that local officials "...are the architects of their own responses to the structural constraints and changing conditions in which city politics is embedded" (Stone, 1987, p. 14). City officials are not viewed as passive reactors, but as independent, albeit bounded, actors influencing local development (Stone, 1987; Jones and Bachelor, 1993). These independent decisions are based on a rational analysis of financial conditions, goals, and risk (Pagano and Bowman, 1989), although perhaps subject to bureaucratic and procedural limits (Lineberry, 1977; Jones et al., 1980; Rubin, 1988; Pagano and Bowman, 1989; Rubin, 1990; Reese, 1993). In this view, "considerable slack exists in the social cables that bind the local polity and the local economy," allowing local leadership the room to shape their own destinies, even in the face of severe economic constraints (Jones and Bachelor, 1993, p. 253).

Macro Discourse

The debate between city limits and city power occurs at both macro and micro levels, with problems of language and unit of analysis. The discussion of power highlights the macro discourse; given the very real limits placed on cities, what is the extent of the power of local officials vis-à-vis the environment, specifically business interests in the case of economic development. The roots of this debate can be traced to early community power studies pitting the elitist and pluralist arguments of Hunter (1953) and Domhoff (1978) against Dahl (1961) and Polsby (1980) respectively.

4

Historically, pluralists argued that political conflict reflected a variety of relatively equal interest groups competing before an independent government answerable to voter demands. Elitists argued that a resource-rich upper class dominated the decisions of elected bodies in their own interests. Both positions, however, reflect a variety of conceptual and empirical deficiencies. Elitism has always suffered from its paranoid flavor and the lack of attention to electoral processes and divergence in interest among elites. Pluralism, on the other hand, has never satisfactorily dealt with issues of limited representation within and resource variation among groups, and strains the concept of government neutrality. Different world views were also influenced by methodological issues such as locale and policy arena examined and technique employed to identify "powerful" participants.

The systemic power contribution of Stone (1980) did much to further the understanding of community power structures. Stone reconciled elitist and pluralist approaches by acknowledging that business leaders have divergent interests and governmental leaders independent powers. However, he argues, the demands of interest groups and citizen coalitions and the need for monetary and political resources from the business community create a situation where official attention to corporate needs is more a function of environmental conditions than overt control.

Currently, regime theory, arguing that coalitions of government officials and business interests form to carry out governmental policy or "social production," reigns supreme (Elkin, 1987; Stone, 1989). Peterson's critique notwithstanding, the prevailing doctrine suggests that politics does matter and that local governments can affect the larger environment.

Micro Discourse

The micro discourse raises a slightly different question. Given that "politics matters," can individuals impact the economic environment? In other words, does leadership matter? These issues were raised in early studies of "great leaders" and policy entrepreneurs (Eyestone, 1978; Mollenkopf, 1983). Subsequent literature has pointed to the influence of individual leaders on their environment and identified the independent effects of leadership under conditions of fiscal stress and revenue raising (Levine et al., 1981; Clark and Ferguson, 1983).

Local government officials are not completely constrained by business elites in this view and can have some impact on their environment. Indeed, "...different leaders with differing abilities, will exploit the situation differently, and different outcomes will be produced" (Jones and Bachelor, 1993, pg. 15). Thus, economic development policies, and ultimately the local economy, can be affected by individual local leaders.

POLITICS VERSUS BUREAUCRACY

If one were looking for true leadership in economic development, where would it most likely be found: in the mayor's or city manager's office or in the office of the director of economic development? In a world where Wilson's

5

(1887) politics/administration dichotomy prevailed, the answer would be clear. The locus of policy-making would rest with elected officials while the job of implementation would fall to bureaucrats.

Much of the literature to date seems to suggest that this is the case. Descriptions of economic development policy-making in major cities from Detroit to Atlanta highlight the role played by elected officials in determining economic development policy (Stone, 1989; Jones and Bachelor, 1993). These cases, however, have several elements in common. They occur in large communities and involve a "big event"--a major new auto plant, a riverfront market or aquarium, or a significant attraction such as the World's Fair. Such situations are often characterized by "peak bargaining," where mayors are central in negotiations with the leaders of a small number of other major interests or "command posts," and "expensive capital projects and issues of current high salience" are involved (Jones and Bachelor, 1993, p. 53).

However, most economic development decisions do not involve "big events." Indeed, Jones and Bachelor suggest that "economic development is a prime candidate for peak bargaining, but only when major projects are contemplated (Much of policy making in the economic-development sphere is as routinized as it is in other areas of policy)" (Jones and Bachelor, 1993, p. 241). Economic development policy activity is a combination of a few "big events" and many routinized decisions and day-to-day actions. And, such routines, often controlled by professionals rather than elected officials, have been found to affect arenas from foreign policy (Allison, 1971) to urban service delivery (Jones et al., 1980). Even in such "mayor-centered" cities as Detroit, the role of development professionals is visible; "in several private developments, city bureaucrats, and in particular the city's economic and development department, were active partners" (Orr and Stoker, 1994, p. 59).

DECISION RULES AND SOLUTION SETS

To the extent that professional actors provide leadership, if only for routine decisions, the nature of their decision-making becomes critical. If peak bargaining, coalition building, and regime maintenance characterize leadership in the electoral sphere, decision rules and standard operating procedures reign supreme in the administrative sphere. Personal attitudes, professional training, past experiences, and the actions of others appear to affect policies and techniques selected and promoted by professionals (Rubin, 1988; Pagano and Bowman, 1989; Rubin, 1990; Reese, 1993). Professional leadership appears to be influenced by turbulence in the environment, producing goal displacement (substituting what is being accomplished for what should be accomplished) and "shooting at anything that flies" (utilizing all possible activities and hoping that something will hit the target) (Reese, 1993).

"The formal and informal arrangements that characterize the regime encourage a particular definition of a city's problems and tend to limit search processes for solutions to those problems" (Jones and Bachelor, 1993, p. 249). What has been done in the past strongly influences what is being done in the present. Thus, to the extent that such decision rule behavior characterizes both bureaucratic decision-making for routine events and regime decision-making for "big events" (referred to as solution sets by Jones and Bachelor), any analysis of local economic development policy-making must take such rules into account.

IN SEARCH OF CROSS-NATIONAL THEORIES

This book has several goals. First, obviously, is the examination of local economic development in a particular cross-national context: the U.S. and Canada. Each case is analyzed individually both to describe what cities are doing and to pursue specific research hypotheses. Then cities in the two nations are explicitly compared against a set of criteria to identify similarities and differences.

Chapter 2 focuses more specifically on the comparative economic development literature to date and identifies three perspectives on the comparison between the U.S. and Canada. The first view is that the two countries are so inherently different in history, social forces, and governmental structure that comparison is rendered impossible, or at least misleading or oversimplified. A second perspective is that the two countries are inherently similar in many important ways; thus, comparisons are appropriate and constructive. Finally, a third viewpoint argues that, while at one time the environment for local governance was extremely different, cities in the two countries are now converging. Thus, comparisons between local policies are becoming increasingly apt. Given this latter view, the question of the appropriateness of the comparison between the two countries is determined by assessing what in fact is happening in a particular policy area.

A second goal relates to assessing what cities are doing in economic development. For many years, the academic literature, even when focusing on a single country, has tended to put the cart before the horse, evaluating economic development techniques without first systematically describing what cities are doing. Most of the literature focuses on the techniques used in a single city, and urban researchers are left knowing only that cities "select an unknown number of development options from their arsenal" (Pagano and Bowman, 1989, pg. 7). One goal of this book, then, is to address this issue by taking a step back and describing in detail what a number of cities of varying sizes and characteristics are doing to foster economic development. Which techniques are most widely employed? Are cities quite similar in policy or is there evidence of innovation and variation? Is economic development primarily an arena for large, economically stressed urban centers? Or is it a common concern for communities across the board?

Several issues relating to the types and mix of economic development mechanisms and policies will also be explored. More specifically, researchers have debated whether cities are still engaging primarily in the "smokestack chasing" policies of the 1970s and 1980s. In other words, are they pursuing a development policy based primarily on attracting industrial concerns from other locations? Or, have cities begun to shift from such supply-side initiatives to more demand-side measures as suggested by Eisinger (1988)? If this is the case, cities should be evidencing policies directed more at business creation than attraction. The sample cities will be analyzed with this distinction in mind to determine if the overall mix of incentives pursued and goals articulated represents a supply- or demand-side approach. Chapters 3 and 4 detail economic development policies, techniques, and mechanisms in Michigan and Ontario cities, representing the U.S. and Canada, respectively. The validity of this particular comparison will be discussed further in Chapter 2.

Addressing these issues cross-nationally is obviously another central goal of the book. There is a paucity of local economic development literature on Canadian cities in particular and U.S. urban scholars have tended to adjust their focus either internally--or more recently--toward Europe. This is disappointing, however, because the U.S./Canada comparison offers compelling prospects for local economic development research. In a "most similar systems" sense, this comparison allows for cross-national exploration within a context of federal democratic systems. The proximate location allows for examination of policy transmission, emulation, and competition.

Still, cultural, historical, and economic differences abound. Do the imperatives of a post-industrial economy and the globalization of markets create uniformity in policy response among cities in the two nations? Or, do national differences refine the reactions of local communities? In short--is there a North American local response to economic stress? Further, do differences in legislative environment affect local policies and might such effects be similar across the border? As will be described in more detail in later chapters, Michigan and Ontario provide very different state/provincial enabling environments, with legislation in the former allowing greater policy discretion to cities. Chapter 5 compares policies across the two nations, noting many points of similarity and several significant differences, and essentially concludes that policy responses in cities in the two countries are indeed converging in many respects.

The aim of this book, however, is larger than a comparison of one local policy arena in two neighboring countries. Ultimately, the goal is to examine and refine current theories of economic development policy-making to include the role of professional bureaucrats and to test an explanatory model which operates cross-nationally. Chapter 6 refines the argument regarding the role of economic development professionals in local policy-making. What really affects local development policy? Is economic development policy totally economistic, as some authors argue? Do cities with high job loss, high unemployment, de-industrialization, and a declining tax base uniformly offer incentives at all cost? Are they most likely to be throwing spaghetti at the wall? Or, do other variables such as governmental structure play a role? What is the relative influence of economic forces, inter-local competition, elected officials, and economic development professionals? Is there a role for rationality and comprehensive planning in local economic development?

8

Chapters 7 and 8 identify and test explanatory models of economic development policy-making raised by such questions. Chapter 7 describes a model of economic development policy-making, including such factors as economic stress, governmental structure, locus of control, and rational planning. Chapter 8 presents an extended model which seeks to explain the economic development policy mechanisms chosen in a given community.

THROWING SPAGHETTI

In comparing local economic development policy and policy-making in two nations, the research reported here provides an opportunity for developing overarching theory. Cross-national research identifies both similarities and differences between two or more societies.

Much past research has tended to overemphasize the effects of national borders. Such work has invariably been designed as a contrasted group sample--a methodology intrinsically appealing for cross-national analysis. In such research, cases are divided into two contrasting groups; in this case, cities in the U.S. and Canada. Any differences between the samples are assumed to be products of the known contrast. This technique tends to assume cause and minimize difference. It also hampers efforts to identify commonalities which can lead to the development of theories of local economic development which operate across borders. While this book begins with a description and analysis of contrasts, it moves to examine variables, actors, and policy processes common to cities in both nations. Thus, it posits and tests the argument that similar post-industrial economic forces affect cities in North America in similar ways. And, given some variance due to historical and social forces, cities in the two nations exhibit similar policy-making processes. To the extent that this is the case, cross-national theories of local economic development policy-making can be developed and tested.

REFERENCES

Allison, G.T. 1971. *Essence of decision: Explaining the Cuban missile crisis.* Boston: Little, Brown and Co.

Bingham, R.D. 1976. *The adoption of innovation by local government.* Lexington, MA: D.C. Heath & Co.

Bowman, A.O'M. 1988. Competition for economic development among southeastern cities. *Urban Affairs Quarterly* 4 (June): 511-527.

Bowman, A.O'M. and Pagano, M.A. 1992. An analysis of the public capital mobilization process. *Urban Affairs Quarterly* 27 (March): 356-374.

Clark, T.N. and Ferguson, L.C. 1983. *City money.* New York: Columbia University Press.

Dahl, R.A. 1961. *Who governs?* New Haven: Yale University Press.

Domhoff, G.W. 1978. *Who rules America now?* Englewood Cliffs: Prentice-Hall.

Eisinger, P.K. 1988. *The rise of the entrepreneurial state.* Madison: University of Wisconsin Press.

Elkin, S. 1987. *City and regime in the American republic.* Chicago: University of Chicago Press.

Eyestone, R. 1978. *From social issues to public policy.* New York: John Wiley.

Hunter, F. 1953. *Community power structure: A study of decision makers.* Chapel Hill: University of North Carolina Press.

Jones, B.D. and Bachelor, L.W. 1993. *The sustaining hand.* Lawrence, Kansas: University Press of Kansas.

Jones, B.D., Greenberg, S. and Drew, J. 1980. *Service delivery in the city: Citizen demand and bureaucratic rules.* New York: Longman.

Kantor, P. 1987. The dependent city the changing political economy of urban economic development in the United States. *Urban Affairs Quarterly* 22 (June): 493-520.

Katznelson, I. 1976. The crisis of the capitalistic city: Urban politics and social control. In W.D. Hawley (eds.) *Theoretical perspectives on urban politics* (214-229). Englewood Cliffs: Prentice-Hall, Inc.

Levine, C.H., Rubin, I. and Wolohojian, G.C. 1981. *Politics of retrenchment.* Beverly Hills: Sage.

Lineberry, R.L. 1977. *Equality and urban politics.* Beverly Hills: Sage.

Mier, R. and Bingham, R.D. 1993. Metaphors of economic development. In R.D. Bingham and R. Mier (eds.), *Theories of local economic development* (284-304). Newbury Park, CA: Sage.

Mollenkopf, J. 1983. *The contested city.* Princeton: Princeton University Press.

10

Molotch, H. and Logan, J.R. 1985. Urban dependencies new forms of use and exchange in U.S. cities. *Urban Affairs Quarterly* 21 (December): 143-170.

Orr, M.E. and Stoker, G. 1994. Urban regimes and leadership in Detroit. *Urban Affairs Quarterly* 30 (September): 48-73.

Pagano, M.A. and Bowman, A.O'M. 1989. Risk assumption and aversion: City government investment in development. Paper presented at the Annual Meeting of the American Political Science Association, Atlanta, GA.

Pelissero, J.P. and Fasenfest, D. 1989. Suburban economic development policy. *Economic Development Quarterly* 3 (November): 301-311.

Peterson, P.E. 1981. *City limits*. Chicago: University of Chicago Press.

Polsby, N. 1980. *Community power and political theory*, 2nd. edition. New Haven: Yale University Press.

Reese, L.A. 1991. Municipal fiscal health and tax abatement policy. *Economic Development Quarterly* 5 (February): 23-32.

Reese, L.A. 1993. Decision rules in local economic development. *Urban Affairs Quarterly* 28 (March): 501-513.

Rubin, H.J. 1988. Shoot anything that flies; claim anything that falls; conversations with economic development practitioners. *Economic Development Quarterly* 3 (August): 236-251.

Rubin, H.J. 1990. Working in a turbulent environment: Perspectives of economic development practitioners. *Economic Development Quarterly* 4 (May): 113-127.

Stone, C.N. 1980. Systemic power and community decision-making: A restatement of stratificationist theory. *American Political Science Review* 74: 978-990.

Stone, C.N. 1987. The study of the politics of urban development. In C.N. Stone and H.T. Sanders (eds.) *The politics of urban development*, (3-22). Lawrence: University Press of Kansas.

Stone, C.N. 1989. *Regime politics: Governing Atlanta*. Lawrence: University Press of Kansas.

Wilson, W. 1887. The study of administration. *Political Science Quarterly* 2: 197-222.

11

CHAPTER 2

POLICY IN CANADIAN AND U.S. CITIES

Cross-national research is important in many respects. Most obviously, it affords the opportunity to develop and test overarching theories of governance and policy-making. Comparisons across national systems allow for the identification of processes, lines of causation, and policies upon which theoretical frameworks can be constructed. In the case of local economic development policy-making, comparisons across post-industrial nations provide a context which includes certain environmental commonalties; specifically, those emanating from the role of cities in the international economic order. Thus, cross-national research allows for an analysis of the operation and effects of common economic changes and stresses.

Cross-national research also provides the means for interpreting differences which may result from different historic or cultural settings, perceptions or definitions of reality, governmental systems, and economic exigencies (Kohn, 1989; Wolman, 1993). In short, comparative analysis should provide the means for differentiating between situations which appear the same but really aren't, or that are the same for different reasons, and ultimately, identify situations which are caused by common forces operating in a similar manner (Wolman, 1993; Fasenfest, 1993).

CROSS-NATIONAL COMPARISONS OF LOCAL DEVELOPMENT POLICY

Cross-national comparisons can provide insights on a variety of issues; alternative problem definitions, causal connections, policy alternatives, governmental differences, and so on (Wolman, 1993). Wolman has specifically suggested seven criteria on which local governments in different nations can be compared: structural environment, extent of problem conditions, problem definition, policy objectives/goals, nature of resources brought to address problems, extent of resources employed, and impact of policies (1993, pgs. 17-18).

To date, such cross-national policy comparisons relating to economic development policy have largely focused on the U.S. and U.K., or to a lesser extent, the U.S. and France and the U.S. and Japan (see for example Molotch and Vicari, 1988; Wolman and Goldsmith, 1992; DiGaetano and Klemanski, 1993; Harding, 1994; Levine, 1994). Most U.S./U.K. comparisons have revealed important variations on some of the criteria noted above, within the context of general similarities. For example, cities in Great Britain are more heavily influenced/affected by national policy initiatives, and are more concerned with employment growth and distributional issues than cities in the U.S., which tend to stress fiscal base and revenue enhancement (Wolman and Goldsmith, 1992; Wolman, 1993). Further, cities in Great Britain evidence less business control or influence on governmental policy, greater non-business political party influence, less decentralization of capital among cities, less reliance on property tax or other "own-source" revenues, and less opportunity to use land acquisition as an economic development tool due to ownership patterns (Hudson and Williams, 1979; DiGaetano and Klemanski, 1993; Harding, 1994).

The literature on France reflects a similar pattern, noting that the greater role of the national government, with concomitant limits on local initiative, and strong parties frame a different environment for local economic development than is the case in the U.S. (Les Gales, 1990; Levine, 1994). Recent research on Berlin points to similar contextual variations; an increased role for political parties and the central government, more codified policy regulations, and a political culture with less emphasis on accumulation of private profit (Strom, 1994).

These differences notwithstanding, the comparative European literature points to growing similarities in local economic development practices, suggesting a theory of convergence. That cities across many industrialized nations are becoming more similar in local economic development is not surprising, given universal trends in the international economic environment. The globalization of local economies, competition between cities, and a desire to preserve jobs and tax base create a "local growth politics that transcends national borders and climates" (Levine, 1994, pg. 406). Other authors have identified the presence of local growth/development coalitions across industrialized countries to a greater or lesser extent (Levine and Vanwelsep, 1988; Molotch and Vicari, 1988; Parkinson, et al., 1993; Harding, 1994; Strom, 1994). Indeed, in Great Britain local governing regimes in the U.S. sense were not directly observable in the past, particularly those including business elements, due to the relatively stronger planning and regulatory powers of the state (Keating, 1991). However, more recent trends suggest that economic development regimes are becoming more prominent, albeit with a somewhat different mix of actors (Stoker, 1988; DiGaetano and Klemanski, 1993). The result appears to be greater effort directed toward local development even at the cost of social goals (MacKintosh and Wainwright, 1988; Parkinson, et al., 1993; Levine, 1994).

COMPARING CANADA AND THE U.S.

Is there a North American city? Researchers from both the U.S. and Canada have argued this question. Are Canadian and U.S. cities basically the same, or, at least, comparable? Or are the two contexts so different that comparative analysis is futile or inappropriate?

Too Many Differences?
A seminal work in this debate by Goldberg and Mercer (1986) contends that the two urban systems are inherently incomparable, primarily as a result of cultural factors. They specifically identify differences in levels of collectivism and interventionism resulting from the distinct history of the Canadian federal system. In fact, they suggest that other work finding similarities between the systems suffers from flawed research techniques or blatant chauvinism. Other authors have also pointed to differences in political culture, the role of the state, and the extent of emphasis on and acceptance of collective definitions of rights (Smart, 1994).

Some aspects of the Canadian urban environment seem to support this view. Canadian cities have not suffered the economic stress and population loss of many U.S. cities (Garber and Imbroscio, 1989; Randall, 1994), perhaps due to lower levels of manufacturing employment (Mercer and Goldberg, 1986). Clearly, the federal systems differ, as Goldberg and Mercer suggest, with disparate impacts on cities. Canadian cities are similar to those in the U.S. in that they lack federal constitutional status, though they may have home rule depending on provincial statutes. Most provinces do not approve individual city charters, but rather adopt uniform charters for classes of cities (Higgins, 1977).

Many traditional urban functions such as police, roads, and education are shared by cities and provinces. Health care, housing and welfare are almost entirely the responsibility of provincial governments (Siegal, 1980; Frisken, 1986). In land regulation, policies regarding zoning, impact fees, and changes in local planning documents often require review by provincial bodies (Higgins, 1977; Goldberg, 1978; Ontario Municipal Board Act, 1980). Thus, cities in Canada are much more dependent upon the will of the individual province than are cities in the U.S. (Smith and Bayne, 1994).

Canadian cities also tend to have fewer direct ties to the national government than their U.S. counterparts (Mercer and Goldberg, 1986; Andrew, 1994). This is particularly evident in intergovernmental aid transfers; only two percent of the local revenue base comes from the federal government (Richmond, 1981). Consequently, most local revenue comes from property taxes, license and permit fees, fines, and in some cities, utility taxes. Canadian cities seem to make greater use of non-tax revenues than U.S. cities, although residents also tend to pay higher property taxes (Mercer and Goldberg, 1986). This more limited intergovernmental revenue tends to restrict independent initiatives on the part of Canadian cities (Higgins, 1977). Further, it has been suggested that Canadian cities evidence less racial segregation, less suburbanization, more regional governance, and higher levels of rational planning (Mercer, 1979; Cullingworth, 1987; Reese, 1993).

Enough Similarity?

These and other differences notwithstanding, many other researchers have conducted comparative studies of U.S. and Canadian cities and argue that such comparisons are wholly appropriate and instructive. Indeed, much past research may have tended to put too much emphasis on differences attributable to the border. Recent research suggests that common post-industrial economic trends create similar policy and governing arrangements for economic development in Canadian and U.S. cities (Turner and Garber, 1994; Reese and Fasenfest, 1994). It appears that cities in the two nations, which share regional and economic base characteristics, also share development ideologies--the growth machine, policies, and a lack of rational planning (Turner and Garber, 1994). In a broad sense, since both are capitalistic and federal systems, it has been suggested that they share a liberal political tradition. Cities in both nations have experienced similar post-industrial trends; an increased importance of the service economy, the pivotal nature of information production and consumption, decreased manufacturing employment, and increased employment in administrative and governmental positions (Levine, 1989; Davies and Donoghue, 1993; Davies and Murdie, 1994). Indeed, Levine speaks of the "globalization of economic life" affecting cities across the North American continent (1989, pg. 141).

Further, the allocation of power to municipalities in Canada is fairly similar to that in the U.S. (Clark, 1985), with provinces adopting many policies toward cities as the states do in the U.S. (Frisken, 1986). In many cases, urban independence in Canada reflects varying provincial policies and regulations, just as it does in the U.S. There is no general pattern indicating that cities in Canada are more limited than those in the U.S. This is particularly visible in areas such as planning (Frisken, 1988). Provinces, like states, control the extent of home rule and policy discretion.

Indeed, many authors have noted that the role of local governments vis-à-vis the provinces and federal government is changing (Smith and Bayne, 1994). Possibilities for and examples of direct federal/urban interaction are growing, particularly for development projects (Artibise and Kiernan, 1989; Leo and Fenton, 1989). Some authors see the desire for cost-cutting and reduced federal governmental roles in Canada leading to a general decentralization of responsibility, necessitating an increased role for cities and more federal attention to urban issues (Davies and Murdie, 1994). Frisken's (1991) description of property tax reforms in the Province of Ontario supports this view, suggesting that local governments are not without power in their relationships with provincial governments.

In the planning function in particular, researchers point to a "climate of change." "One important manifestation of this change, perhaps the most important, has been a deliberate and pronounced shift in favor of local control, both in the structure of planning systems and in their regular operations" (Smith and Bayne, 1994, pg. 726). These authors predict increased local initiative and control in planning, more attention to specific local needs within

16

plans, less standardization and regional control, less technical rationality, and more avenues for citizen input. This appears to be part of a general shift from rationality in policy-making to sensitivity to "political" concerns, bringing Canadian cities closer to their U.S. counterparts (Aucoin, 1986; Leo and Fenton, 1989).

Even with respect to intergovernmental transfers, it appears that practices in Canadian and U.S. cities may be converging. Nowlan (1994) finds that intergovernmental aid patterns in Canada closely reflect those in the U.S., with large increases in the percentage of local revenue from transfers from 1958 through the late 1970s, followed by a reduction of federal transfers and more pressure on the provinces during the 1980s. Such reductions seem to stimulate similar local revenue reactions, including increased reliance on user fees, development levies, and local-area improvement charges (Nowlan, 1994).

CONVERGENCE IN LOCAL ECONOMIC DEVELOPMENT POLICY

Many comparisons of Canadian and U.S. urban economic development focus on the role of land in development and ask whether or not a "growth machine" exists in Canada (Molotch, 1976). Do land-based interests such as developers, landowners, bankers, and realtors push for development to increase profits? Such pressures stimulate local officials to pursue a program of growth, typically through numerous economic development incentives. Work by Lorimer (1972), Sancton (1983), and Turner and Garber (1994) certainly seem to reveal such growth-machine dynamics across time periods in Canadian cities.

Indeed, cities in Canada practice a variety of economic development incentives (Sancton, 1983; Leo and Fenton, 1989; Reese, 1992). Though Canadian cities have not experienced the severity of economic downturn of many U.S. cities, some have had to deal with a substantial loss of financial base (Filion, 1987) and exhibit increasing structural unemployment. Significant disparities exist across Canada in income and economic activity; smaller cities are less well off, for example (Gertler and Crowley, 1977). Central cities in both countries have experienced population loss, although in the past the situation has not been as extreme in Canada as in the United States (Mercer and Goldberg, 1986). More affluent residents stayed in the central city in Canada while middle- and lower-class residents live in outlying suburbs (Goldberg and Mercer, 1980; Ley, 1988).

However, recent research on Canadian cities indicates a continuing loss of central city population and consequent financial stress (Davis and Murdie, 1994). Indeed, many authors suggest that in such trends central cities in Canada are merely lagging behind those in the U.S. (Schnore and Peterson, 1958; Mercer, 1979; Randall, 1994). ·Like their U.S. counterparts, there appears to be significant central city deterioration relative to the suburbs (Nathan, and Adams, 1989). Canadian central cities are losing population relative to suburbs, central city income levels are lower and unemployment higher, and poverty exists at higher levels (Randall, 1994), with increasing concentrations of the poor in urban areas (Davis and Murdie, 1994). It also appears that the "edge city" phenomena is occurring in Canada despite provincial controls, less freeway development, and higher levels of planning (Garreau, 1991).

Canadian cities practice a variety of economic development techniques, including financial incentives/inducements (Lorimer, 1972; Whelan, 1989), development of quasi-public redevelopment corporations (Leo and Fenton, 1989), and direct municipal investment (Artibise, 1988). Although Ontario provincial regulations limit financial incentives, other provinces--Alberta, for example--allow wide discretion for cities in financial matters (Bettison, Kenward, and Taylor, 1975).

Competition for economic development is also salient for Canadian cities. Although important variations exist between provincial governments, many allow cities to compete for development fairly autonomously. In fact, one author suggested that the provincial government "leaves the local authorities subject to the conflicting influence of their private investors, developers, and industrialists, etc., on the one hand and the public requiring expensive amenities on the other" (Bettison, Kenward, and Taylor, 1975, pg. 491). Indeed, in an account of development in Toronto, Stein (1972) painted a picture very familiar to U.S. urbanists of developers obtaining large concessions from cities and variances in land-use plans to secure much desired development. In a similar vein, case studies of cities in both nations portray a development policy driven by the needs of private interests rather than long term "rational" planning (Levine, 1989; Turner and Garber, 1994).

The U.S.-Canada Free Trade Agreement appears to have increased competition between cities across the border. As Roberts and Smith note, "...the new decision-making environment [for firms] will more closely resemble that of a Michigan producer trying to decide whether to locate or expand in Ohio or Indiana than that of a firm deciding whether to compete in international markets" (1992, pg. 53). And, while cities in Ontario, for example, have fairly wide discretion in levying "development charges" on developers to balance the cost of infrastructure improvements and population pressures, uncertainty over future costs typically results in increased fees and tax burdens on current residents and businesses (Sancton and Montgomery, 1994). This situation, too, is very similar to many in the U.S., where the push for additional development often creates a variety of unintended social costs for current residents.

In summary, it appears that even given some important differences, the comparison between the U.S. and Canada is viable and important in several respects. While the federal systems create similarities in social and economic relationships, Canada also shares many characteristics with European countries--the relative preeminence of planning, the power of the state, and the population density of central cities (Goldberg and Mercer, 1986; Feldman and Goldberg, 1987). "As a result Canada may offer the possibility of the combination of 'most similar systems' and 'most different systems' comparative analysis that Pickvance (1986) suggests can be very productive"

(Smart, 1994, pg. 573). This review of both the Canadian/U.S. and European/U.S. literature highlights a pattern of convergence in so far as local economic development and related planning issues are concerned. In short, while important systemic and cultural differences continue to exist, the globalization of capital production and competition and the need for local tax base and jobs has made economic development a preeminent activity for many municipalities across nations. For economic development policy, at least, external forces appear to create "similar systems" even in different contexts.

THE CURRENT COMPARISON

Although much of the literature on economic development has focused on central cities and/or larger municipalities, cities of all sizes engage in economic development practices. A more complete analysis that includes smaller and/or suburban units provides a broader picture (Pelissero and Fasenfest, 1989). Given that there is significant variation among cities in levels of economic development, it is reasonable to examine practices across a wide group of municipalities (Fainstein et al., 1983; Logan and Molotch, 1987). While the goal is to explore economic development practices in a range of cities, the lack of existing literature argues against complete national comparison in favor of more indepth analysis of a more focused set of cities.

The Sample

The Province of Ontario and the State of Michigan were selected for analysis for a variety of theoretical and practical reasons. Selecting cities in a single state and province controls for variation in enabling legislation and the general climate for economic development strategies. For Ontario, this is particularly important since previous research indicates that competition for economic development in Canada is as much a provincial as a local phenomenon. Further, research has suggested significant variations in public opinion orientations and identities across the provinces, with an increasing "provincialization" of identity (Tuohy, 1992). Thus, studying cities in one province and one state will control for such competition and emerging identity, and permit a focus on intercity competition and variation (Sancton, 1983).

The Michigan/Ontario comparison was selected for several additional reasons. Their proximity to each other is important, increasing the likelihood that similar techniques will be employed, perhaps by diffusion and competition between cities. Ontario also serves as the location for much of Canada's industrial and manufacturing interests. Cities there should reflect the most extensive use of economic development practices (Goldberg and Mercer, 1986). Further, of Canada's most populated 28 cities, most are located in Ontario (Artibise, 1988); indeed, by 1981, almost 82% of Ontario's population was considered urban (Frisken, 1986). Because Ontario is home to the majority of U.S.-owned enterprises in Canada (Gertler and Crowley, 1977), cities in Ontario may be more similar to U.S. cities, particularly those in the Midwest, than to others in Canada for comparative purposes.

19

Cities in Ontario also appear to have experienced levels of economic stress more similar to U.S. cities, particularly those in the rust-belt, than other cities in Canada. Recent research on population loss and economic stress indicates that of the eight most severely deteriorated cities in Canada, seven are located in the Province of Ontario (Randall, 1994).

The selection of Michigan and Ontario does, however, require a caveat. Since the environment for cities in Ontario and Michigan is quite similar, i.e., more of the nature of the "similar systems" approach, such a sample may limit generalizations to cities in more diverse areas with less competition and interaction. However, it is reasonable to believe that the Ontario/Michigan comparison provides a good picture of local economic development policy and policy-making under conditions of "rust-belt" economic stress, while still including cities of varying sizes, governmental arrangements, and even fiscal health.

The Survey

A questionnaire was sent to economic development directors, planners, city managers/administrators, and mayors in all municipalities in the Province of Ontario with designations as "cities"; this classification includes most municipal units with populations over 15,000 (N = 49). The same officials were sent surveys in all cities in the State of Michigan with populations over 10,000 (N = 89). The survey was designed to conform to one developed by the International City/County Management Association for cities across the United States. The specific questions were developed after a series of face-to-face interviews with local economic development officials. While these interviews were critical in developing a valid instrument, responses themselves were very enlightening and have been incorporated into the text where appropriate. Interviews were also conducted with local community and economic development officials subsequent to the mail survey to explore particular issues and relationships.

Surveys were mailed in the fall of 1990. Response rates for chief executives--mayors and managers--were extremely low and few planners had responsibility for economic development. Thus, the analysis presented here is based on responses from economic development officials, with some comparison made to other groups where appropriate. After two mailings, response rates for economic development officials were quite high for Ontario (86%), while slightly lower for Michigan (61%). Both of these rates represent responses significantly above the 20-40% range considered "average" for mailed surveys (Nachmias and Nachmias, 1992).

The surveys for the two nations varied only slightly in terminology and economic development techniques employed to reflect known differences in governmental structure and policy. Survey questions were developed through face-to-face interviews with economic development officials and other governmental actors in both countries. Questionnaires were designed to elicit information on a variety of topics including the mix of different economic development techniques and mechanisms employed, governmental and local economic development structural arrangements, resources devoted to the economic development effort, professionalism, locus of control and initiative, goals, perceptions of competition and other environmental features, decision-making criteria, planning and evaluation methods, and various demographic characteristics. Thus, the survey lends itself to comparison on a number of the criteria identified by Wolman, including structural environment, goal definition, resource allocation and policy selections. Further, it allows for exploration of decision-making procedures and power relationships between actors.

The following chapters describe economic development policies and procedures for each set of cities. However, to avoid redundancies in presentation and provide an organizing framework to the discussions, specific hypotheses are presented and tested for both sets of cities. These hypotheses revolve around central issues in the economic development literature and highlight differences in the policy-making environment in the two nations.

For example, some authors have suggested that cities are shifting their approach to economic development, moving from incentives designed to attract mobile capital (supply-side) to those intended to create capital from within the community (demand-side) (Eisinger, 1988). Such a shift is posited regardless of such environmental issues as enabling legislation and levels of economic stress and competition. Michigan cities operate in a framework of extremely liberal state enabling legislation, particularly in the area of taxing and spending, and are located in a traditional "rust-belt" environment. Given these conditions, is the trend toward policies which stress local resources and the development of indigenous business still occurring? This issue is pursued in the next chapter as current economic development policies in the state are described.

Ontario and Michigan cities differ in the extent of state/provincial restrictions on local discretion regarding economic development incentives. Ontario imposes more limits on the ability of cities to use financial incentives. Chapter 4 explicitly examines the effects of differences in such enabling legislation. Whether such differences have an impact on the types of policies cities employ and whether it promotes a shift to demand-side policies is explored. Thus, this chapter addresses the effects of different enabling environments. Since Ontario cities share the same "rust-belt" location and have similar industrial investments as Michigan cities, do they pursue the same mix of economic development incentives? Or, does the difference in enabling legislation have some mitigating impact? These questions are addressed as the economic development mechanisms used in Ontario cities are described.

Finally, Chapter 5 provides a direct comparison of economic development strategies and incentives in Ontario and Michigan. The discussion is organized around several specific points of comparison and ends with some thoughts regarding the issue of policy convergence between cities in the two nations.

REFERENCES

Andrew, C. 1994. Federal urban activity: Intergovernmental relations in an age of restraint. In F. Frisken (ed.), *The changing Canadian metropolis: A public policy perspective* (427-457). Berkeley: Institute of Governmental Studies Press and Toronto: Canadian Urban Institute.

Artibise, A.F.J. 1988. Canada as an urban nation. *Daedalus* 117 (Fall): 237-264.

Artibise, A.F.J. and Kierman, M.J. 1989. *Canadian regional development: The urban dimension.* Ottawa: Economic Council of Canada, Local Development Paper No. 12.

Aucoin, O. 1986. Organizational change in the machinery of Canadian government: From rational management to brokerage politics. *Canadian Journal of Political Science* 19 (March): 3-28.

Bettison, D.G., Kenward, J.K., and Taylor, L. 1975. *Urban affairs in Alberta.* Edmonton, Alberta: University of Alberta Press.

Clark, G. 1985. *Judges and the cities: Interpreting local autonomy.* Chicago: University of Chicago Press.

Cullingworth, J.B. 1987. *Urban and regional planning in Canada.* New Brunswick: Transaction Books.

Davies, W.K.D. and Donoghue, D.P. 1993. Economic diversification and group stability in an urban system: The case of Canada, 1951-1986. *Urban Studies* 70 (7): 1165-1186.

Davies, W.K.D. and Murdie, R.A. 1994. The social complexity of Canadian metropolitan areas in 1986: A multivariate analysis of census data. In F. Frisken (ed.), *The changing Canadian metropolis: A public policy perspective* (203-236). Berkeley: Institute of Governmental Studies Press and Toronto: Canadian Urban Institute.

DiGaetano, A. and Klemanski, J.S. 1993. Urban regimes in comparative perspective: The politics of urban development in Britain. *Urban Affairs Quarterly* 29 (September): 54-83.

Eisinger, P.K. 1988. *The rise of the entrepreneurial state.* Madison: University of Wisconsin Press.

Fainstein, S.S., Fainstein, N., Hill, R.C., Judd, J. and Smith, M.P. 1983. *Restructuring the city.* New York: Longman.

Fasenfest, D. 1993. Local economic policy formation: Setting an agenda for development research. In D. Fasenfest (ed.), *Community economic development: Policy formation in the U.S. and U.K.* (3-13). London: Macmillan and New York: St. Martin's Press.

Feldman, E. and Goldberg, M. 1987. *Land rites and wrongs.* Cambridge, MA: Lincoln Institute of Land Policy.

Frisken, F. 1986. Canadian cities: The American example: A prologue to urban policy analysis. *Canadian Public Administration* 29 (Fall): 345-376.

22

Frisken, F. 1988. *City policy-making in theory and practice*. London: University of Western Ontario, Local and Regional Government Program.

Frisken, F. 1991. The contributions of metropolitan government to the success of Toronto's public transit system: An empirical dissent from the public-choice paradigm. *Urban Affairs Quarterly* 27 (December): 268-292.

Garber, J. and Imbroscio, D. 1989. Canadian federalism and economic development: The myth of the North American city reconsidered. Paper presented at the annual meeting of the American Political Science Association, Atlanta, GA.

Garreau, J. 1991. *Edge city: Life on the new frontier*. New York: Doubleday.

Gertler, L.O. and Crowley, R.W. 1977. *Changing Canadian cities: The next 25 years*. Toronto: McClelland and Stewart.

Goldberg, M.A. 1978. The BNA Act, NHA, CMHC, MSUA, etc...: 'Nymophobia' and the on-going search for an appropriate Canadian housing and urban development policy. In M. Walker (ed.), *Canadian confederation at the crossroads* (320-361). Vancouver: The Fraser Institute.

Goldberg, M. and Mercer, J. 1986. *The myth of the North American city: Continentalism challenged*. Vancouver: University of British Columbia Press.

Harding, A. 1994. Urban regimes and growth machines: Toward a cross-national research agenda. *Urban Affairs Quarterly* 29 (March): 356-382.

Higgins, D.J. 1977. *Urban Canada: Government and politics*. Toronto: Macmillan Canada.

Hudson, R. and Williams, A.M. 1979. *Divided Britain*. London: Bellhaven.

Keating, M. 1991. Local development politics in France. *Journal of Urban Affairs* 13: 443-459.

Kohn, M. 1989. Cross-national research as an analytical strategy. In M. Kohn (ed.), *Cross-national research in sociology*. London: Sage Publications.

Leo, C. and Fenton, R. 1989. Intervention by indirection: Urban development corporations and the politics in Canadian city centers. Paper presented at the annual meeting of the Urban Affairs Association.

Les Gales, P. 1990. Local economic policies, the state and city councils: Coventry and Rennes. In D.S. King and J. Pierre (eds.), *Challenges to local government* (122-144). London: Sage.

Levine, M.A. 1994. The transformation of urban politics in France: The roots of growth politics and urban regimes. *Urban Affairs Quarterly* 29 (March): 383-410.

Levine, M.A. and Van Weesep, J. 1988. The changing nature of Dutch urban planning. *Journal of the American Planning Association* 54 (Summer): 315-323.

Levine, M.V. 1989. Urban redevelopment in a global economy: The cases of Montreal and Baltimore. In R.V. Knight and G. Gappert (eds.), *Cities in a global society* (141-152). Newbury Park: Sage.

Ley, D. 1988. Social upgrading in six Canadian inner cities. *Canadian Geographer* 32 (1): 31-45.

Logan, J.R. and Molotch, H.L. 1987. *Urban fortunes: The political economy of place.* Berkeley: University of California Press.

Lorimer, J. 1972. *A citizens guide to city politics.* Toronto: Lorimer.

Mercer, J. 1979. On continentalism, distinctiveness, and comparative urban geography: Canadian and American cities. *Canadian Geographer* 23 (2): 123.

Mercer, J. and Goldberg, M.A. 1986. Value differences and their meaning for urban economic development in Canada and the U.S. In G.A. Stelter and A.F.J. Artibise (eds.), *Power and place* (343-394). Vancouver: University of British Columbia Press.

Mercer, J. and Goldberg, M.A. 1980. Canadian and U.S. cities: Basic differences, possible explanation, and their meaning for public policy. Papers of the Regional Science Association 45: 175.

Molotch, H. 1976. The city as a growth machine. *American Journal of Sociology* 2: 302-330.

Molotch, H. and Vicari, S. 1988. The development process in the United States, Japan, and Italy. *Urban Affairs Quarterly* 24 (December): 188-214.

Nachmias, C.F. and Nachmias, D. 1992. *Research methods in the social sciences.* New York: St. Martin's Press.

Nathan, R.P. and Adams, C.F. 1989. Four perspectives on urban hardship. *Political Science Quarterly* 104 (Fall): 483-508.

Nowlan, D.M. 1994. Local taxation as an instrument of policy. In F. Frisken (ed.), *The changing Canadian metropolis: A public policy perspective* (799-841). Berkeley: Institute of Governmental Studies Press and Toronto: Canadian Urban Institute.

Ontario Municipal Board Act Revised Statutes of Ontario 1980. Chapter 347. Ministry of Attorney General.

Parkinson, M., Bianchini, F., Dawson, J., Evans, R. and Harding, A. 1993. *Urbanisation and the functions of cities in the European community.* Brussels: European Commission.

Pelissero, J.P. and Fasenfest, D. 1989. Suburban economic development policy. *Economic Development Quarterly* 3 (November): 301-311.

Pickvance, C.G. 1986. Comparative urban analysis and assumptions about causality. *International Journal of Urban and Regional Research* 10: 162-184.

Randall, R. 1994. U.S. and Canadian urban vitality a metropolitan analysis. Paper presented at the annual meeting of the Urban Affairs Association, New Orleans, LA.

24

Reese, L.A. 1992. Local economic development practices in the province of Ontario. *Canadian Public Administration* 35: 237-249.

Reese, L.A. 1993. Local economic development across the northern border. *Urban Affairs Quarterly* 28 (June): 571-592.

Reese, L.A. and Fasenfest, D. 1994. Local economic development policy in a cross-national context: Canadian and U.S. border cities. Paper presented at the annual meeting of the American Political Science Association, New York.

Richmond, D. 1981. Provincial-municipal tax and revenue sharing: Reforms accomplished, 1978 compared with 1971. In L.D. Feldman (ed.), *Politics and government of urban Canada* (4th ed.) (162-201). Toronto: Methuen.

Roberts, K. and Smith, P.R. 1992. The effect of labor cost differences on the location of economic activity under the U.S.-Canada Free Trade Agreement. *Economic Development Quarterly* 6 (February): 52-63.

Sancton, A. 1983. Conclusion: Canadian city politics in comparative perspective. In W. Magusson and A. Sancton (eds.), *City government in Canada* (291-317). Toronto: University of Toronto.

Sancton, A. and Montgomery, B. 1994. Municipal government and residential land development: A comparative study of London, Ontario, in the 1920's and the 1980's. In F. Frisken (ed.), *The changing Canadian metropolis: A public policy perspective* (777-798). Berkeley: Institute of Governmental Studies Press and Toronto: Canadian Urban Institute.

Schnore, L.F. and Peterson, G.B. 1958. Urban and metropolitan development in the United States and in Canada. *Annals of the American Academy of Political and Social Science* 316: 60-68.

Siegal, D. 1980. Provincial-municipal relations in Canada: An overview. *Canadian Public Administration* 23 (Summer): 281-317.

Smart, A. 1994. Recent development in the theory of the state and the changing Canadian metropolis: Implications of each for the other. In F. Frisken (ed.), *The changing Canadian metropolis: A public policy perspective* (561-579). Berkeley: Institute of Governmental Studies Press and Toronto: Canadian Urban Institute.

Smith, P.J. and Bayne, P. 1994. The issue of local autonomy in Edmonton's regional plan process: Metropolitan planning in a changing political climate. In F. Frisken (ed.), *The changing Canadian metropolis: A public policy perspective* (725-750). Berkeley: Institute of Governmental Studies Press and Toronto: Canadian Urban Institute.

Stein, D.L. 1972. *Toronto for sale*. Toronto: New Canada Press.

Stoker, G. 1988. *The politics of local government*. London: Macmillan.

Strom, E. 1994. In search of the growth coalition: American urban theories and the redevelopment of Berlin. Paper presented at the annual meeting of the American Political Science Association, New York.

Tuohy, C.J. 1992. *Policy and politics in Canada*. Philadelphia: Temple University Press.

Turner, R.S. and Garber, J.A. 1994. Responding to boom and bust: Urban political economy in Houston and Edmonton. Paper presented at the annual meeting of the American Political Science Association, New York.

Whelan, R.K. 1989. Urban redevelopment in Montreal: A comparative, North American perspective. Paper presented at the annual meeting of the Urban Affairs Association.

Wolfe, D. 1989. The Canadian state in comparative perspective. *Canadian Review of Sociology and Anthropology* 26: 95-126.

Wolman, H. 1993. Cross-national comparisons of urban economic programmes: Is policy transfer possible? In D. Fasenfest (ed.), *Community economic development: Policy formation in the U.S. and U.K.* (14-42). London: Macmillan and New York: St. Martin's Press.

Wolman, H. and Goldsmith, M. 1992. *Urban politics and policy.* Cambridge: Blackwell.

CHAPTER 3

ECONOMIC DEVELOPMENT POLICIES IN MICHIGAN CITIES[1]

As noted in Chapter 1, research on local economic development policies has suggested that the types of techniques employed in cities were changing in the early 1990s. Specifically, Eisinger noted that "subnational economic development policy has undergone a recent shift from an almost exclusive reliance on supply-side location incentives to stimulate investment to an approach that increasingly emphasizes demand factors in the market as a guide to the design or invention of policy" (1988, pg. 10). Supply-side efforts are directed at lowering the cost of doing business in a particular location, thus attracting more mobile capital investment. The major effect is to move capital from place to place. Demand-side activities, on the other hand, are designed to encourage and foster the development of new business or capital. This is done primarily by stimulating demand for local goods and promoting risk-taking by indigenous entrepreneurs (Eisinger, 1988).

Eisinger's conclusions regarding this shift to demand-side policies were based on several case studies and national data from large cities. Little research, however, has examined whether cities generally are embracing such techniques. The sample of Michigan cities will be examined to address this issue, pursuing two questions;

- What types of economic development incentives or mechanisms are employed? and,
- Are cities shifting to "demand-side" practices?

SUPPLY- VERSUS DEMAND-SIDE POLICIES

Many studies have identified common local economic development practices, including subsidizing business, informing and exhorting prospective developers, regulating and/or impacting crucial industries and institutions, expanding market opportunities, shaping market structure, limiting forms of enterprise, and operating public enterprises or expanding public employment opportunities (Sternberg, 1987). While the possible array is extensive, the number widely practiced is few. Some of the most often employed techniques appear to be tax incentives/abatements, site acquisition/preparation, industrial revenue bonds, efforts to rebuild and improve the downtown, public relations and boosterism, and investment in infrastructure (Wassall and Hellman, 1985; Matulef, 1987; Pelissero and Fasenfest, 1989; Reese, 1991).

As noted previously, Eisinger has reduced the various economic development techniques into two categories; supply and demand oriented activities. Supply-side incentives include all types of tax or incentive systems, debt-financing schemes, infrastructure investment, labor incentives, regulatory policy, tax increment financing arrangements, enterprise zones, and land and site development. Demand-side incentives include business incubators, venture capital financing, research and development support, targeting of incentives, small business support, and job creation strategies (Eisinger, 1988, pg. 12).

The key to this typology lies in Eisinger's analysis of the underlying goals of supply and demand oriented policies. Supply-side techniques have in common the goal of economic growth by reducing the costs of production in a specific community. Several characteristics follow from this central premise:

- economic growth results from attracting mobile firms from outside the locality;
- each city competes with others for this mobile capital;
- cities should thus try to attract any or all industries possible, though perhaps avoiding very risky ventures; and,
- governmental action should be directed at reducing the costs of production for private firms rather than intervening in private sector "decisions about where to invest, what businesses will be profitable, and what products will sell" (Eisinger, 1988).

Demand-side techniques rest on an entirely different set of assumptions. The central goal of these techniques is economic growth through local markets, promoting development or expansion of indigenous firms and spurring local demand for products and services so such expansion can take place. Thus, government plays an active role in developing and identifying markets or firms and aids in the creation or expansion of local firms, often focusing on the start-up stage. Such activities can only take place after development goals are clarified, markets and firms studied, and a strategic plan created to allow the "establishment of long-term economic goals that may realistically be met" (Eisinger, 1988. pg. 27).

Eisinger's primary thesis, presented in The Rise of the Entrepreneurial State, is that there is an "environmental transformation" occurring in economic development policy. In his view, transformation has produced the shift from widespread reliance on supply-side techniques to demand-side policies. Eisinger identifies four major changes behind this transformation, summarized below.

1) As cities in the northern and midwestern U.S. began to lose population and industry to the south and west, the initial conclusion was that local costs of production must be lowered to recapture a competitive edge. The resulting supply-side incentives led to increased competition and had

little impact when widely and uniformly employed. Thus, cities have turned to demand-side policies.

2) Cuts in federal aid to cities have forced a reliance on local resources, leading officials to focus on growth potential within the local economy.

3) The increasing importance of international markets has led cities to identify and target local products or services with a competitive export edge for policy support.

4) The shift to a service economy and concomitant loss of manufacturing employment has led cities to target development efforts on industries and firms promising future growth.

These motivating forces assume that cities have not only recognized economic changes but have acted rationally by substituting one set of policies for another. Eisinger highlights the drawbacks of supply-side incentives: they tend to be effective only at the margins; they tend to relocate investment rather than build it; tax incentives are unwieldy, promote intercity competition, and lower revenue bases; and the effectiveness of incentives is reduced as more cities and states offer them. Demand-based policies are seen as preferable because they create a positive sum game. They ostensibly create new capital investment, direct resources toward growth industries which are often based on new and innovative technology, and reduce competition between states and cities.

The analysis of advantages and disadvantages is reasonable and in some cases is supported in the literature. It is unclear, however, that local officials have responded with the purported policy transformation. It remains to be seen empirically whether cities are actually changing the types of techniques employed to reflect a demand orientation.

Indeed, several constraints facing local officials suggest wariness in accepting Eisinger's argument. First, many of the demand-side incentives described by Eisinger are appropriate only for state governments, which possess greater resources and regulatory powers and have the ability to support such things as development credit corporations, product-development corporations, venture capital corporations, export-promotion programs, and plant-closing laws. This limits the likelihood of local usage. Second, in addressing the issue of why local governments continue to use tax incentives in the face of a body of evidence suggesting minimal effectiveness at high cost, Wolman (1988) suggests that officials rationally may continue such policies for several reasons. Tax incentives may still be widely employed because they are visible and symbolic efforts that let citizens and businesses feel that something is being done. Further, since it remains unclear whether such incentives work, it is better to gamble that they do than to avoid them and have them work for neighboring cities. Finally, other research suggests that economic development officials select policies for reasons other than a rational analysis of effectiveness. Rubin (1990) notes a tendency on the part of local officials to try all possible economic development techniques because of uncertainty about what will work and political pressure to show visible results.

Thus, it is expected that, as a result of uncertainty and an unwillingness or an inability to change to demand-side incentives, Michigan cities will not evidence the shift from supply to demand-side policies posited by Eisinger.

DEFINING POLICY TYPES

Specific questions in the survey were used to distinguish between demand or supply side strategies based upon Eisinger's typology. Supply-side activities included such strategies as tax abatements, loans, loan guarantees, industrial revenue bonds (IRB's) and less restrictive regulatory policies.

Demand-side policies were somewhat more difficult to measure partly because they are newer and less codified in practice. But, demand-side policy also represents as much an orientation to development as a laundry list of activities. Further, as previously mentioned, many of Eisinger's demand-side techniques revolve around venture capital, often only feasible for the largest cities and state governments.

Because many demand-side policies are directed at stimulating local small business and promoting economic base diversity, local officials were explicitly asked whether these were primary economic development goals. Conversely, if a city saw attracting new business as a primary goal, that would indicate a supply-side mentality. Further, because of the centrality of strategic planning to demand-side targeting of incentives, economic development directors were asked if they had an economic development plan, if there was a structured system to evaluate achievement of economic development goals, and whether systematic approaches such as cost/benefit analysis or forecasting were employed to evaluate possible economic development incentives or projects. Absent these factors, it would be hard to argue that the planning elements to support demand-side policies were in place. Officials were also asked if they pursued "all types of economic development incentives allowed by the state" and whether the city "usually grants any incentives requested by firms." Positive responses to these items would indicate an absence of the targeting implicit in demand-based initiatives.

As with supply-side strategies, city officials were asked if they engaged in various demand-side activities; specifically, development of export markets, market development planning, business incubators, training funds or programs, business liaison committees, and office/retail or industrial property management. These strategies conform to Eisinger's demand-side policy type. The development of export markets for local goods was explicitly mentioned by Eisinger as a demand-side policy, as was the formation of business incubators. The related activity of property management places the city in the position of entrepreneur, providing locations for fledgling firms. While Eisinger classifies training as a supply-side technique, this is true only if efforts are directed at the narrow needs of one firm considering relocation. When general training and education result in a more highly skilled work force, start-up of new enterprises is facilitated. Under these circumstances, training more closely fits the demand-side model and is considered such in this research.

PROFILE OF MICHIGAN CITIES

A brief description of the Michigan cities included in the sample is instructive in analyzing economic development practices (see Table 3-1). An interesting point at the outset is that the majority of respondents felt that their cities have been prospering economically; indeed, nearly two thirds stated that the local economy had experienced at least some growth. Only 15% of the respondents indicated declining economies, with most of these indicating modest rather than significant declines. For almost half of the cities, the predominant economic base is industrial, with just over a quarter primarily residential.

In terms of structure, economic development activities are most likely to be implemented by an economic development division which is part of a larger department, such as community development or planning. The next most likely arrangements include fragmenting economic development functions among several departments or placing economic development functions under the direction of the city manager. The use of a free-standing department devoted solely to economic development or vesting economic development responsibility in an external commission are less prevalent. Given the importance of economic development noted in the academic literature, the small number of cities utilizing an independent department is surprising.

More than half of the cities have a city manager form of government and another fifth have a mayor and a city manager. Over a third have a mayor/council form of government. Michigan's "reformed" government traditions are clearly in evidence here.[2] Nonpartisan elections predominate among cities in the state.

Just over a third of Michigan cities have a formal economic development plan, and such plans are strongly affected by the needs and desires of the private sector. Indeed, plans were most likely developed through business needs surveys and consultant studies. However, input from community advisory committees was solicited and open meetings held with the community in almost half of the cities with development plans. While elected neighborhood commissions are used infrequently, citizen surveys were employed 29% of the time. Only a fifth of the cities indicated that there was no formal means for citizen input into the economic development planning process. Much of this input may be stipulated by federal and state guidelines, and there appears to be no effort to measure the efficacy of citizen input. However, it is clear that some effort is made to take the views of interests other than business into account when making economic development plans in the state.

In summary, the majority of cities involved in the Michigan sample are economically expanding, or at least economic development officials perceive them to be expanding. City manager systems predominate and the economic development function is generally located in a larger city department, typically community development. Economic development planning, where it exists, is most likely driven by business needs and external consultants with some input by citizens.

To describe the types of economic development mechanisms employed in Michigan cities and assess whether they appear to be embracing demand-oriented policies, survey responses regarding development practices over the past five years were analyzed. City officials were asked whether they had employed each of a list of different economic development mechanisms at any time over the five-year period. To simplify analysis and presentation, incentives have been divided into five general categories; marketing techniques, governance tools and infrastructure development, governmental regulations, land and property management, and financial tools. These categories are based on those used in a 1985 survey of U.S. cities conducted by the International City/County Management Association (Appendix B contains a complete listing of techniques by category). The following section describes the techniques most commonly used in each category and also identifies the primary goals for economic development held by local officials and the extent of rational planning and evaluation taking place.

INCENTIVES AND STRATEGIES EMPLOYED

Marketing Techniques

Marketing techniques include those activities which are primarily aimed at promoting awareness of what a city has to offer to prospective businesses. They are heavily used by Michigan cities. The most widely used marketing tool, 83%, is an inventory of available sites which can then be presented to prospective firms for promotional purposes (see Table 3-2). Several other techniques in the category are also practiced by over half of the cities; the production of brochures, visits to prospective firms, and the promotion of specific development sites. These marketing efforts can be quite elaborate. Thus, a "brochure" sent to a prospective firm may well contain information on local population demographics, labor force characteristics, airport services, state tax structure, local millage rates, local housing market characteristics, utility rates, public school achievement scores, technology resources, and characteristics of local development sites.

While not employed by a majority of cities, trade show attendance is also fairly widespread, as is the use of liaison committees between government and business to facilitate development. Smaller numbers of cities attempt to solicit foreign business interests, use videos to promote the city, have a marketing development plan (28%), or stress the development of export markets for local goods. However, everything is relative, and even these less commonly used marketing techniques are employed in over a quarter of the cities.

Governance Tools/Infrastructure

This category of techniques includes governmental policies to improve city infrastructure or services such as parking, traffic circulation, garbage collection, water treatment, and so on. They are designed to make the locality more desirable for business location (see Table 3-3). A majority of cities focus efforts on improving the infrastructure base of the city, including aesthetic improvements, parking, pedestrian amenities, recreation facilities, and traffic circulation. Indeed, almost two thirds of the sample cities have used such improvements to spur economic growth. Cities also tend to rely heavily on improvements in sewage collection/treatment, street cleaning and garbage collection, water treatment/distribution, and the development of community improvement areas. All the techniques within this category are employed in over one third of the cities.

Governmental Regulations

Techniques in this category revolve around governmental regulation and include measures that ease restrictions or limit bureaucracy such as one-stop permit procedures or creation of an ombudsperson. Fewer techniques in this category are used in the majority of the cities surveyed (see Table 3-4). Indeed, only one is used by over half of the cities, improved or streamlined building inspection procedures. Less common practices include a modified zoning process to facilitate changes necessary for development, and the use of an ombudsperson to smooth relations between the private and public sectors. Relatively few cities have consolidated the permit process to reduce red tape or relaxed environmental regulations to spur development.

Land and Property Management

These practices revolve around the use of land as a basis for economic development and some tend to be quite heavily used by cities in Michigan (see Table 3-5). Three practices are employed by a majority of cities; sale of land to developers, land acquisition, and clearing land of unusable structures. Several other techniques are widely used as well, including consolidating available lots and developing city-owned industrial parks.

Many of the land management techniques identified by the survey-- business relocation, leasing of land to developers, donation of land to developers, management of industrial property--are employed by only small numbers (11 to 19%) of cities. Even less commonly used incentives include enterprise zones, management of office/retail interests by the local government, and land expropriation.[3]

Financial Tools

Some of the techniques in this category are among the most heavily practiced economic development activities (see Table 3-6). Tax abatement is the most common incentive; with 83% of the cities in Michigan offering some type of abatement, it ties with an inventory of available development sites for the most heavily used technique overall. Tax Increment Financing Authorities

(TIFA) and Downtown Development Authorities (DDA) are also widely used. Clearly these three types of incentives are a major component of economic development in Michigan cities.

Other financial incentives are also fairly common. Bonds are issued for economic development in 39% of the cities, and various types of loans--direct, subsidies, and guarantees--are offered by at least one fifth of the cities. The offer of in-kind services is much less common, as is the use of the other financial tools.

Economic Development Goals

Economic development directors were not likely to see major demand-side goals as top priorities, although some mixed messages were present. The goal most often mentioned as guiding economic development was the retention and expansion of existing business. However, this more likely represents a desire not to lose current firms rather than an effort to stimulate new local business expansion. Just under a quarter of respondents identified economic base diversity as a top goal, and a mere 7% identified small business development as being a number one priority.

More common economic development goals were downtown development, the attraction of new business, and industrial development. This suggests that cities are trying to keep what economic base they have while downplaying goals which would stimulate demand through base diversity and small business development.

Strategic Planning

As previously mentioned, only 38% of the cities have a formal economic development plan. Since plans are absent, it is not surprising to find that few cities use any formal systematic process to evaluate whether economic development goals are being achieved. Only 16% use cost/benefit analysis or some other system to evaluate prospective economic development options. On the other hand, majorities of respondents agree that the city pursues all types of incentives allowed by law, and indicate that the city usually grants all incentives requested.

What is evident here is a group of cities lacking the strategic planning and targeting processes identified as so necessary by Eisinger to carry out demand-side policies. The resultant tendency is to use all techniques possible in the hope that something will lure prospective industries; in the words of Rubin (1988), "shooting at anything that flies."

ARE MICHIGAN CITIES EMBRACING DEMAND-SIDE POLICIES?

Overall, Michigan cities do not seem to be embracing demand-side strategies to any significant extent (see Table 3-7). Supply-side incentives are still widely employed. While business liaison committees are fairly common (44%), only 28% of the cities have a plan for market development, and only 15% attempt to develop export markets for local goods. Nineteen percent of Michigan cities have business incubators and only 7% have acted as

34

entrepreneurs in retail or office property management. Slightly more have engaged in industrial property management. Finally, only 11% of the cities report the use of training funds or programs.

The ten most common economic development practices in Michigan are identified in Table 3-8. When presented in this manner, the predominance of supply-side financial incentives becomes apparent. Tax abatements and TIFA's are first and third among all techniques. And, while marketing techniques figure predominantly as a group, only the use of promotional brochures ranks near the top, employed by 70% of cities. Visits to prospective firms and compiling information on available sites rank ninth. Infrastructure techniques also rank high, with 6 among the top 10.

In short, it appears that cities in Michigan rely heavily on traditional supply-side techniques. While the survey provides only cross sectional data, demand-side techniques would rate more highly if cities in the state had been moving to embrace them during the last half of the 1980s.[4] Indeed, data from a more narrow study of economic development efforts in Michigan in 1988/1989 suggested that the same techniques predominated then (Reese, 1991).

Demand-side techniques, such as training programs, business incubators and export market development, are employed by only a small number of cities across the state. Indeed, incubators rank twenty-fourth, export development ranks twenty-sixth, and training ranks twenty-seventh among all economic development techniques employed.

Clearly, Eisinger's contention that cities are shifting to demand-side initiatives does not appear to hold true for cities in Michigan. Classic supply-side techniques predominate. Few cities employ demand-side incentives designed to promote the creation and growth of local smaller businesses. Strategic planning and targeting, central facets of a demand-side strategy, are almost absent in Michigan. It should be noted, however, that interviews with Michigan officials and previous research (see Reese, 1994) suggest that such targeting may be more likely to occur at the county or regional level than within cities.

As has been noted previously in the literature, Michigan cities appear typical in their focus on financial, marketing, site acquisition and infrastructure techniques, although it is possible that such reliance is more extreme in this state than others (Wassall and Hellman, 1985; Sternberg, 1987; Pelissero and Fasenfest, 1989; Reese, 1991). Indeed, it appears that Michigan cities are much more likely to use tax abatements than U.S. cities generally--83% as opposed to 34% in states allowing tax abatements. This appears to be the case for TIFA's as well; 68% as opposed to 29% (Sharp and Elkins, 1991). Because many of the more innovative demand-side initiatives noted by Eisinger are most feasible at the state level, it could be that cities have not found ways to adapt such schemes. In the face of numerous questions about the effectiveness of supply-side incentives, and the promise suggested by demand-side activities, it is a matter of concern that cities across a "rust-belt" state such as Michigan appear to continue to widely embrace

35

supply-side initiatives. The lack of economic development planning and limited evaluation of current and prospective techniques may potentially explain this reliance and adds to the general concern.

The next chapter describes economic development techniques practiced in Ontario cities using the same categories of techniques employed here. Further, it examines what the academic literature has to say about differences in enabling legislation and assesses the effects of the Ontario regulatory environment. It concludes with some thoughts about practices in Ontario cities, specifically addressing the question of whether more restrictive provincial legislation leads cities in Ontario to employ more demand-side practices than in Michigan.

TABLE 3-1
Michigan Sample Characteristics (N=54)

Description of Local Economy	%
Rapid expansion (more than 25% growth)	09
Moderate growth (10%-25%)	35
Slow growth (less then 10%)	30
Stable	11
Modest decline (less than 10%)	11
Significant decline (more than 10%)	04

Predominant Economic Base	%
Industrial	48
Residential	26
Commercial	14
Totally mixed	07
Institutional	04
Agricultural	00

Governmental Structure	%
City Manager	56
Mayor/Council	37
Mayor/Manager	20

Structure of Economic Development Function	%
Within a Larger Department	33
Functions carried out by several departments	19
Under city manager	17
Separate government department	15
Outside commission	13
Other	02

Economic Development Plan
Yes 38%
No   62%

Table 3-1 (continued)

Methods Used to Develop Plan	%
Business needs survey	57
Consultant studies	54
Community advisory committee	47
Open meetings	43
State agencies	39
Special interest advisory groups	36
Evaluation of existing facilities	32
Analysis of local data	29
Citizen survey	29
Other	07
Elected neighborhood commissions	04

TABLE 3-2

Marketing Techniques	% Practicing
Inventory of available sites	83
Brochures	70
Visits to prospects	52
Promote specific sites	52
Trade shows	32
Solicit foreign business	26
Videos	26

TABLE 3-3

Governance Tools and Infrastructure Investments	% Practicing
Aesthetic improvements	65
Improved/expanded parking	65
Improved pedestrian amenities	63
Improved/expanded recreation facilities	61
Improved traffic circulation/streets	61
Improved sewage collection/treatment	43
Improved street cleaning/garbage collection	37
Improved water treatment/distribution	35
Community improvement areas	33

TABLE 3-4

Governmental Regulations	% Practicing
Improved building inspection	63
Modified zoning process	35
Ombudsperson	30
Consolidated/one-stop permits	17
Relaxed environmental regulations	02

TABLE 3-5

Land and Property Management	% Practicing
Sale of land to developers	70
Land acquisition	63
Clearing structures	54
Lot consolidation	41
City-owned industrial parks	39
Business relocation	19
Leasing land to developers	19
Donating land to developers	11
Enterprise zones	07
Land expropriation	06

TABLE 3-6

Financial Tools	% Practicing
Tax abatements	83
Tax Increment Finance Authority	68
Downtown Development Authority	60
Issuance of bonds	39
Loan subsidies	28
Direct loans to business	28
Loan guarantees	24
In-kind services	17
Sale-lease back arrangements	11
Deferred tax payments	11
Donations of unused real property	07

TABLE 3-7

Demand-Side Techniques	% Practicing
Business liaison committees	44
Market development planning	28
Business incubators	19
Industrial property management	15
Develop export markets	15
Training funds/programs	11
Office/Retail property management	07

TABLE 3-8
Most Commonly Used Techniques

Rank	%Practicing	Activity
1	83	Tax abatements
2	70	Brochures
	70	Sell land
3	68	Tax Increment Finance Authority
4	65	Improved parking
	65	Aesthetic improvements
5	63	Pedestrian amenities
	63	Improved building inspection
	63	Acquire land
6	61	Improved traffic circulation
	61	Improved recreation
7	60	Downtown Development Authority
8	54	Clear land
9	52	Visits to prospects
	52	Inventory of specific sites
10	43	Improved sewage collection

1. An earlier version of this analysis was published as Local Economic Development in Michigan: A Reliance on the Supply-side, *Economic Development Quarterly*, 6 (November 1992): 383-393.

2. Percentages do not total 100 for forms of government because separate questions were used for each type of governmental format. Chief executive types exceed 100% because some respondents may have indicated both a manager and a mayor/manager structure.

3. It should be noted that although 7% of the cities indicated use of enterprise zones, under state law only one city was eligible for an enterprise zone at the time of the study.

4. Respondents were asked if their cities had engaged in any of the techniques during the last five years.

REFERENCES

Eisinger, P.K. 1988. *The rise of the entrepreneurial state.* Madison: University of Wisconsin Press.

Matulef, M.L. 1987. Strategies for economic revitalization. Paper presented at the National Conference of the American Society for Public Administration, Boston, MA.

Pelissero, J.P. and Fasenfest, D. 1989. Suburban economic development policy. *Economic Development Quarterly* 3 (November): 301-311.

Reese, L.A. 1991. Municipal fiscal health and tax abatement policy. *Economic Development Quarterly* 5 (February): 23-32.

Reese, L.A. 1994. The role of counties in local economic development. *Economic Development Quarterly* 8 (February): 28-42.

Rubin, H.J. 1988. Shoot anything that flies; claim anything that falls; conversations with economic development practitioners. *Economic Development Quarterly* 3 (August): 236-251.

Rubin, H.J. 1990. Working in a turbulent environment: Perspectives of economic development practitioners. *Economic Development Quarterly* 4 (May): 113-127.

Sharp, E.B. and Elkins, D.R. 1991. The politics of economic development policy. *Economic Development Quarterly* 5 (May): 126-139.

Sternberg, E. 1987. A practitioner's classification of economic development policy instruments, with some inspiration from political economy. *Economic Development Quarterly* 1 (May): 149-161.

Wassall, G. and Hellman, D. 1985. Financial incentives to industry and urban economic development. *Policy Studies Review* 4 (May): 626-640.

Wolman, H. 1988. Local economic development policy: What explains the divergence between policy analysis and political behavior? *Journal of Urban Affairs* 10: 19-28.

ECONOMIC DEVELOPMENT POLICIES IN ONTARIO CITIES AND ENABLING LEGISLATION[1]

The previous chapter identified an apparent contradiction in local government choices regarding economic development techniques. To reiterate, Eisinger (1988) and others clearly suggest that demand-side techniques, designed to encourage and foster new development or capital, are superior to supply-side alternatives in promoting economic development. Similarly, Warner (1987) concludes that policies designed to improve the local human capital base and promote the development of high technology firms and general quality of life have a greater impact on growth in per capita income than supply-side efforts to reduce costs to firms. Despite the strong support in both the academic and professional literature for demand-side incentives, it appears that few cities are using such techniques (Wolkoff, 1992). Indeed, this conclusion is supported by the Michigan data.

Is this same contradiction present among Ontario cities? Are Ontario cities using the same types of supply-side techniques widely employed in Michigan? While convergence theories described in Chapter 2 would suggest that cities in both nations tend to stress supply-side techniques, the different provincial legislative environment might affect the mix of policies pursued by Ontario cities, or at least the emphasis on certain supply-side mechanisms. The literature on enabling legislation, focusing predominantly on the U.S., suggests that there may be some differences between Michigan and Ontario cities due to variation in local discretion, and that supra-level legislation will have some affects on local policy.

THE ROLE OF STATE STATUTES

The academic literature suggests that more restrictive state enabling environments, particularly those limiting financial incentives and regulating the relocation of businesses, may reduce deleterious intercity competition (Jones and Bachelor, 1984), and encourage some demand-oriented strategies (Reese and Malmer, 1994). State and provinces can balance the needs of localities, citizens, businesses, and other levels of government by becoming the "policy conduit for power and resources" in local economic development (Stevens and McGowan, 1987, pg. 566).

While there has been limited research on the interaction between state enabling legislation and local economic development policy, work in other policy areas has produced mixed findings. However, the consensus appears to be that state law can significantly affect local policy. Although McManus and Thomas (1979) found local annexation policy to be little affected by state legislation, Dusenbury (1980) and Galloway and Landis (1986) found enabling legislation to be important in explaining local annexation activity, size of communities, and other structural issues. Further, state enabling legislation can standardize local general assistance programs (Albritton and Brown, 1986), while state centralization of fiscal matters can increase local dependency (Stonecash, 1985). In short, it appears that state law can impact local behavior in areas from finance to welfare.

This literature suggests an interesting framework for analysis of economic development policy in Ontario cities since provincial enabling legislation differs significantly from that in Michigan. While, *a priori*, state/provincial enabling legislation restricting the use of certain financial incentives should reduce local use of incentives, the issue of policy trade-offs remains open to debate. Will cities prohibited from using tax abatements, for example, be similar to other cities except for that activity? Or, will they utilize other incentives, and if so, which ones? In short, do differences in enabling legislation affect the balance between supply and demand-side activities in cities? One essential difference between cities in Ontario and Michigan is the provincial restrictions on financial incentives, and it is instructive to examine what happens when higher levels of government become more active in restricting local development practices.

PROFILE OF ONTARIO CITIES

The history of provincial control of local practices in Ontario has been one of gradual restriction. At one time a fairly wide range of financial incentives or "bonuses" was allowed and practiced. As early as 1871, financial incentives were practiced for railways and manufacturing. In the early 1890s, cities were already competing for industry using bonuses (Bucknall, 1988).

In 1924, the Bonuses Limitation Act was passed, limiting fixed assessments (tax abatements) to ten years and requiring three-quarters vote of city council and consent from established industries. In 1962, such abatements were prohibited completely under the Municipal Act. This act also prohibited loans of either property or money, loan guarantees, leasing or selling public property to business below fair market value, and giving exemptions for any fees, levies, or other charges (Bucknall, 1988). The only exception to these restrictions is aid to small businesses, to whom cities may sell and/or lease property below market value. Grants can also be given to non-business entities such as nonprofit or quasi-public bodies, and bonuses are allowed for historic preservation (Bucknall, 1988). This essential difference in enabling legislation serves as the backdrop for an examination of local economic development policies among cities in Ontario.

As in Michigan, most respondents felt that their cities have been prospering economically; 88% reported that the local economy had grown at least to some degree over the last five years (see Table 4-1). Indeed, respondents from only two cities said that their local economy had experienced a modest decline; no respondents indicated a significant decline. The predominant economic base in over half of the sample cities is industrial, commercial or mixed use is most common in the rest of the cities.

Economic development activities tend to be carried out by free-standing city departments devoted to that purpose. Indeed, this is the case in well over half of the communities. Fewer cities relied on external economic development commissions and a city department assigned multiple functions was employed in only a couple of cities. On average, there are one to three persons working solely on economic development in each city. Thus, economic development organizations are relatively small.

City governmental structures are predominantly mayor/council, although city administrator/manager and mayor systems are also common. Just a handful of cities have a board of control system. Ward-based city council elections predominate and all elections are nonpartisan.[2]

An impressive number of cities in Ontario have a formal economic development plan, far more than is the case in Michigan. This is likely the result of the 1946 Planning Act which "strongly encouraged municipalities to adopt 'official plans'" (Sancton and Montgomery, 1994, pg. 779). The Planning Act passed in 1983 contains the same emphasis on formal plans. Cities tend to have developed their plans through input from special interest groups--downtown merchants and top industry officials for example--analysis of local data on needs and economic projections, and input from provincial agencies. Far less use was made of citizen surveys or elected neighborhood commissions. While plans are prevalent, citizen input is not; 43% of respondents indicated that citizens had no formal input into the economic development decision-making process whatsoever.

Further, even given the widespread existence of development plans, only 36% of the cities use any type of formal systematic process to evaluate whether economic development goals are being achieved. Fewer use cost/benefit analysis or some other system to evaluate prospective economic development options.

Economic development officials were most likely to identify promotion of economic base diversity as their primary economic development goal, although attracting new business and retaining current firms were also identified as a number one priority in many cities. Far less important as economic development goals were the development of small business, service sector growth, and promotion of minority business; over half of the respondents suggested that these were not goals of their economic development efforts.

In summary, most of the cities in the sample are economically expanding. The major development goals, diversifying the economic base and attracting and retaining industry, are included in a formal economic development plan and pursued by a specialized city department. The city administrator form predominates along with nonpartisan ward-based city council elections. Little formal evaluation of economic development techniques appears to take place either prospectively or retrospectively, and the community at large seems to have minimal input into economic development decision-making.

INCENTIVES AND STRATEGIES EMPLOYED

The dynamics of the economic development policy process in Ontario were succinctly summarized by one local official; "Simplistically, what's driving the process (of economic development) here is the basic desire of municipalities for industrial assessment. They are constantly wooing the commerce and industry to come and locate in their municipality. That's what is driving it." The description of mechanisms employed in Ontario cities reflects the same five general categories used in the previous chapter.

Marketing Techniques

Marketing techniques include those activities which are primarily aimed at promoting awareness of what the city has to offer to prospective and existing businesses. The most widely used marketing tool is the distribution of brochures or promotional material (see Table 4-2). This is the only technique that is practiced by all of the cities in the sample. A video format is often used for promotional literature. Participation in trade shows and visits to prospective firms are done in almost all cities, indicating that marketing is more than just a passive act of distributing literature.

Most cities target foreign businesses with special promotional activities and provide an inventory of possible development sites to interested parties. Both of these activities are conducted by most of the cities. Somewhat fewer are pursuing the development of export markets for local goods. Special promotions for particular development sites and the use of special events to promote business location are employed in a majority of the cities.

A majority of the economic development officials also indicated that business liaison committees were employed. Such committees are typically composed of governmental officials and representatives from a particular industry or commercial area. While part of their function is to serve as a communication link, they also transmit information about the city to other similar businesses. Finally, the majority of cities are pursuing these marketing techniques under the guidance of a codified plan for marketing development.

There were no marketing techniques mentioned in the survey that were practiced by less than half of the cities. Twelve percent of the respondents identified additional techniques not listed in the survey, including visits to existing businesses, business seminars, direct mailings and "power breakfasts."

Governance Tools/Infrastructure

This category includes governmental policies to improve city infrastructure or services such as parking, traffic circulation, garbage collection, water treatment, and so on (see Table 4-3). Somewhat surprisingly, many of the cities noted improved or expanded recreation facilities to promote economic development.[3] Transportation improvements are also widely employed; two thirds to three quarters of the cities had improved pedestrian amenities (plantings, benches, etc.) and traffic circulation, expanded parking, and made aesthetic improvements to promote business development.

Service areas which have been improved by over one half of the cities include sewage collection/treatment and water treatment/distribution systems. Sixty percent of the cities have established community improvement areas for service and infrastructure upgrading. Improved street cleaning and garbage collection services and the establishment of incentives for historic preservation are less widely used, however. Seventeen percent of economic development officials noted other activities in this area not addressed by the survey, including waterfront development, improved access to major highways, and improved educational facilities.

Governmental Regulations

Techniques in this category revolve around governmental regulations and include measures that either ease restrictions (such as height and density variances and one-stop permit procedures) or increase restrictions to better promote development (anti-litter campaigns, sign control and industrial zoning). Fewer techniques in this category are used in the majority of the cities surveyed (see Table 4-4). Industrial zoning,[4] design regulations for industrial parks, sign control regulations, and improved building inspection procedures are the most common practices, employed in over half of the cities. It is interesting to note that most of these activities tend to increase restrictions rather than reduce or ease them.

Less common regulatory practices include height and density variances,[5] facade control regulations, a modified zoning process, a consolidated one-stop permit system, and an ombudsperson to help businesses resolve problems with the city. Even fewer cities have adopted anti-litter regulations to improve the visual desirability of the city for business location or campaigns, have adopted historic district regulations, or have engaged in density transfers.[6] And, no cities indicated that they had relaxed environmental regulations or procedures in order to attract development.

However, cutting red tape appears to be a common theme. One official stated: "From a procedural or process viewpoint, of course, we bend over backwards to be as cooperative as we can with them (business); in other words, to cut through red tape as quickly as we can...whenever approvals are required at our level or at any other level of government, we try to get those through very quickly...because time, of course, is money to industry."

47

Land and Property Management

These practices revolve around the use of land as a basis for economic development and do not appear to be widely used by cities in Ontario (see Table 4-5). Only three techniques are used in over half of the cities; establishing city-owned industrial parks, land acquisition, and sale of city-owned land to developers. Far fewer respondents report managing industrial property or consolidating lots for building development.

The rest of the land management techniques identified by the survey--relocation of businesses to development areas, land expropriation, clearing land of unusable structures, lease arrangements with developers, and rehabilitation of buildings--are practiced by less than one fifth of the sample. None of the cities engage in office or retail property management. One city identified a technique not mentioned in the survey, feasibility studies on specific development sites (probably more of a promotional tool).

It appears that land development strategies vary depending upon the amount of vacant land available for development and property available for redevelopment. In cities with significant land resources, economic development practices focus on purchase, consolidation, and site preparation. Industrial parks are also used in these circumstances, although they are just as likely to be privately as publicly owned.

Cities lacking available land pursue slightly different strategies. Ontario annexation (or "boundary adjustment") procedures are much more flexible than Michigan's, allowing land-poor cities to annex land from surrounding areas, contingent on a provincial hearing rather than on voting in both cities, as is the case in many states such as Michigan. The process works much like a labor settlement procedure with fact-finding, reconciliation, and arbitration. For other cities, options are limited to the redevelopment of land used for other purposes, such as rail and shipping yards, parking structures, or abandoned buildings. Overall, because of provincial restrictions on many financial incentives, land based strategies appear relatively more important in Ontario. More will be said about this later.

Financial Tools

Financial incentives are strictly limited by the Ontario provincial government. Tax abatements were not included in the survey because they are specifically prohibited. While some of the other techniques are illegal, they were included on the survey because in pre-survey interviews some officials indicated that they were practiced in some cities. Given the provincial restrictions, it is surprising to note that all of the techniques mentioned are practiced in at least one city, even though many respondents indicated that all were prohibited. Clearly, financial techniques are not widely practiced; none are employed by more than 50% of the sample (see Table 4-6). The most common techniques in this area are awards for private industry achievement, employee training and retraining funding or programs,[7] support of business incubators, and provisions for assisted housing.[8]

Even with provincial restrictions, a few cities offer loan guarantees (although two cities noted that these were federally funded), use loan subsidies, allow deferred tax payments, and provide direct loans to private businesses, utilize sale-lease back arrangements, offer in-kind services (e.g., public works crews assisting in land clearance), and donate unused real property.[9] Finally, slightly more cities give awards for research initiatives by non-profit groups and identified financial incentives not included in the survey, such as provincial and federal grants and building design awards.

Targeting Economic Development

"Targeting" of economic development policies also seems to be an important strategy in Ontario. Many authors have suggested that cities should identify or target industries which need resources the city has to offer, such as a trained work force or current infrastructure (Hill, 1984; Bingham and Blair, 1984; Rubin and Zorn, 1985). Cities with an overabundance of offices and service industries specifically should avoid attracting banking and insurance interests, for example. Indeed, one city's economic development plan states that "activities targeted toward the financial and business services sector have indeed been relatively limited, consisting primarily of providing assistance and information to businesses requesting it." An official from that city indicated that "office, banking, finance, insurance and so on has tended to look after itself without a lot of support from the city." More creative, smaller scale employers such as the fashion and movie industries are targeted in this case.

Other cities provide counseling to prospective firms to ensure a good match with the location, or promote industrial skills and infrastructure already available. As one official said, "We don't want people to come here on bad information and die in here later." Another city specifically identifies "niche firms" which provide specialized products, do not require a lot of space, and will employ people with skills already available. "Traded sectors" are also likely targets. A traded sector brings outside money into the city, similar to Peterson's concept of export industries (1981), or replaces some imported product. "Non traded sectors" tend to be those in which local businesses are already operating, so incentives would only harm existing enterprise.

THE ROLE OF THE PROVINCE

The provincial prohibition on financial incentives not only influences the economic development techniques practiced, but the level and nature of intercity competition for development as well. While there is considerable competition between Ontario cities (as one respondent stated, "...we are in competition with everybody, all over the place, all the time"), such competition does not appear to reach levels experienced in U.S. cities. Further, many officials see the real competition for Ontario cities in Michigan cities and cities in other border states such as Buffalo, New York. Typical comments include: "...our stiffest competition is from the midwestern states, including Michigan for example, because of their industrial revenue bond program, their abatement programs"; "our main competition is with the Toledo's, the Dayton's, the southern states."

Officials tended to see the lack of restrictions on financial incentives in border states, tax abatements in particular, as a major problem, putting them at a comparative disadvantage in attracting business. However, some respondents acknowledged that restricting financial incentives in Ontario was beneficial in reducing competition. One official stated that they don't feel as pressured by Ontario cities ". . .because they live under the same constraints as we do."

Tax abatement regulations in particular are something officials may not want to include in the "relaxation" of provincial regulations. One official commented: "We feel, once you start that game, there's no end to it, because you just start bidding downward. I've seen some articles written in the states, where some municipalities have come to the point of view that they have just sold themselves out . . .We don't really want to get into that game." "I think it's good that we don't have tax abatements because you end up slicing each other's throat, you get one neighbor against the other neighbor," said another.

Essentially, provincial restrictions do not eliminate competition between cities but serve to ameliorate it. As one official summarized: "We definitely are (in competition with other cities in Ontario) but it is not a head on thing where we are bashing one another or anything of that nature. But, certainly, there are companies that are looking at us and they will also be looking at other cities at the same time." While many economic development officials acknowledge that provincial restrictions limit their ability to compete with other cities, particularly those in the U.S. (52% agree), they are almost evenly split over whether such restrictions are too extreme (40% feel they are too restricted, 43% feel that they are not).

It would be incorrect to conclude from this that intercity competition is nonexistent in Ontario, however. Competition does exist, but of a different nature than that which occurs among Michigan cities. In Michigan, cities compete by individually offering incentives to business in a free market situation. In Ontario, city competition occurs at the provincial level; instead of competing for business attention, they compete for provincial attention.

Financial incentives are not absent in Ontario, they are just prohibited for cities. The province often offers abatements or other financial inducements for particular projects. Cities compete at the provincial level to get the province to provide incentives for their projects. Similarly, variances in provincial rules or limits on city policy, known as special legislation, may be required for certain projects.

Cities lobby the provincial government for such treatment through their members of parliament, mayors and development officials. Other research confirms this competition. Garber and Imbroscio (1989, p.18) state that "...the key to understanding land politics in urban Canada lies in a shift in the locus of growth machine-like activity upwards."

DOES ENABLING LEGISLATION MAKE A DIFFERENCE?

Two general conclusions can be drawn from this analysis. First, it is clear that provincial restrictions on the use of financial incentives have a number of impacts. Cities appear to turn to demand-side methods to attract development. Such techniques tend to be those touted in the literature as more cost effective for cities in the long run. Second, intercity competition is limited by such restrictions, allowing the province to better target development efforts and reducing the ability of private firms to play cities off against one another. Some officials explicitly indicated that they felt more powerful in dealing with business because of the provincial restrictions. One suggested that if a city has to offer a wide package of incentives, there must be something wrong with it anyway: "When you get too good a deal from a municipal government, there is something wrong with that municipality . . . there will be long term hidden costs (for business) you are not aware of."

Further, it is clear that urban economic development practices in Ontario tend to cluster in certain categories. The most widely and consistently used practices are in the category of marketing. On average, nine out of eleven techniques are practiced by the cities surveyed. Governance tools and infrastructure investments are also fairly widely employed, with an average of six out of ten uniformly used. Governmental regulations, land and property management activities and financial tools are less widely employed, with averages of five of thirteen, four of eleven, and two of twelve techniques practiced by all cities respectively. In total, cities in Ontario employ an average of 25 of the economic development techniques listed. The ten most widely practiced techniques across all categories are identified in Table 4-7. Again, marketing activities figure predominantly. However, land based strategies and initiatives such as land acquisition, industrial zoning and industrial parks, and infrastructure improvements also are important.

It appears that cities in Ontario use a range of economic development strategies which conforms closely to those widely practiced by other cities. Marketing, site acquisition, and infrastructure improvement are among the most commonly used techniques according to the literature (Wassall and Hellman, 1985; Sternberg, 1987; Matulef, 1987; Pelissero and Fasenfest, 1989; Reese, 1991). Indeed, because much of the literature focuses on cities in the United States, this research also suggests that similar economic development strategies are employed by cities in Canada and the United States. However, financial incentives such as tax abatements, loans and loan guarantees are notable by their absence in Ontario cities.

Does the limitation on bonuses impact economic development practices in the other categories? In other words, what appears to be the result of the provincial restrictions on bonuses? Based on survey results and personal interviews with a small sample of economic development officials in Ontario, it does seem that restrictions have had some impact. While common techniques do center in the marketing and land based categories, it appears that Ontario cities are also more likely to use more innovative means of attracting economic development. For example, business incubators and training programs are utilized by over 25% of the cities. These techniques, often promoted in the literature as more advantageous to cities (Knight and Gappert, 1984; Jones and Vedlitz, 1988) seem to be used more widely in Ontario than in other cities (Reese, 1991). Regulations to limit or control certain facets of development also seem more prevalent than easing governmental regulations to promote development. Finally, some innovative techniques such as awards for research and development are also evident.

The next chapter explicitly compares Ontario and Michigan cities on a variety of factors pertinent to local economic development. Specific points of comparison follow those suggested by Wolman (1993), including government structure, problem conditions, problem definition, policy goals, resources, and policies employed. Chapter 5 also revisits the debate regarding national differences and the possible convergence between cities in Canada and the U.S., at least regarding economic development. Ultimately, the argument is made that cities in the two nations are remarkably similar in both orientation to and implementation of economic development practices.

TABLE 4-1
Ontario Sample Characteristics (N=42)

Description of Local Economy	%
Rapid expansion (more than 25% growth)	29
Moderate growth (10%-25%)	33
Slow growth (less then 10%)	26
Stable	07
Modest decline (less than 10%)	05
Significant decline (more than 10%)	00

Predominant Economic Base	%
Industrial	55
Commercial	17
Totally mixed	10
Resource	07
Institutional	07
Residential	02
Agricultural	02

Governmental Structure	%
Mayor/Council	88
Mayor/Administrator	55
Mayor/Manager	12
Mayor/Board of Control	05
Ward	43
At-large	24

Structure of Economic Development Function	%
Separate government department	60
Outside commission	19
Within a Community Development Department	07
Other	07
Under city manager/administrator	05
Functions carried out by several departments	02

Economic Development Plan
   Yes 67%
   No   33%

Table 4-1 (continued)

Methods Used to Develop Plan	%
Special interest advisory groups	55
Analysis of local data	45
Consultant studies	43
Provincial agencies	41
Business needs survey	38
Community advisory committee	35
Evaluation of existing facilities	35
Other	17
Citizen survey	10
Elected neighborhood commissions	05
Open meetings	02

**Structured System to Evaluate Movement
Toward Development Goals**

Yes 36%
No 64%

	Priority		
Economic Development Goals	1st	2nd	3rd
Economic base diversity	42	20	12
Attract new business	39	36	15
Retain/expand existing business	36	23	21
Industrial development	30	15	13
Downtown development	08	14	06
Small business development	08	19	03
Tourism/conventions	06	09	23
Office development	03	13	10
Neighborhood commercial dev.	00	09	06
Service sector growth	00	11	14
Minority business development	00	10	07

TABLE 4-2

Marketing Techniques	%Practicing
Brochures	100
Trade shows	98
Visits to prospects	95
Solicit foreign business	93
Inventory of available sites	93
Videos	79
Promote specific sites	74
Business liaison committees	67
Specific events planning	60
Develop export markets	57
Market development planning	55
Other	12

TABLE 4-3

Governance Tools/Infrastructure	% Practicing
Improved/expanded recreation facilities	88
Improved pedestrian amenities	79
Improved traffic circulation/streets	76
Aesthetic improvements	74
Improved/expanded parking	67
Improved sewage collection/treatment	64
Community improvement areas	60
Improved water treatment/distribution	57
Improved street cleaning/garbage collection	38
Incentives for historic preservation	33
Other	17

TABLE 4-4

Governmental Regulations	% Practicing
Industrial zoning	88
Design requirements for industrial parks	79
Sign control regulations	60
Improved building inspection	55
Height and density variances	43
Facade control regulations	38
Modified zoning process	36
Consolidated/one-stop permits	21
Ombudsperson	21
Anti-litter regulations	19
Historic district regulations	12
Density transfers	05
Relaxed environmental regulations	00
Other	00

TABLE 4-5

Land and Property Management	% Practicing
City-owned industrial parks	86
Land acquisition	81
Sale of land to developers	62
Lot consolidation	38
Industrial property management	24
Business relocation	19
Land expropriation	17
Clearing structures	17
Leasing land to developers	14
Rehabilitation of buildings	05
Other	02
Office/retail property management	00

TABLE 4-6

Financial Tools	% Practicing
Awards for industry achievement	33
Training/retraining funds/programs	29
Business incubators	26
Assisted housing	24
Other	12
Sale-lease back arrangements	10
Loan guarantees	07
Awards/funding for research	07
In-kind services	05
Donations of unused real property	05
Deferred tax payments	02
Loan subsidies	02
Direct loans to business	02

TABLE 4-7
Most Commonly Used Techniques

Rank	% Practicing	Activity
1	100	Promotional literature
2	98	Trade shows
3	95	Visits to prospects
4	93	Inventory of sites
	93	Solicit foreign business
5	88	Improve recreation facilities
	88	Industrial zoning
6	86	Industrial parks
7	81	Land acquisition
8	79	Videos to prospects
	79	Pedestrian amenities
	79	Design for industrial parks
9	76	Improved traffic circulation
10	74	Aesthetic improvements
	74	Promote specific sites

1. This chapter is based on earlier work published as Local Economic Development Practices in the Province of Ontario, *Canadian Public Administration*, 35 (Summer 1992): 237-249, and Economic Development Strategies in Ontario: A Comparative Perspective, *The American Review of Canadian Studies* (Summer 1992): 215-233.

2. Percentages do not total 100 because separate questions were used for each type of governmental form and not all cities responded to each structural type.

3. This should be considered with some caution. Because information on recreational and other improvements were self-reported and not independently confirmed, some self-promoting may be taking place.

4. Industrial zoning in Ontario means that land is zoned exclusively for industrial use. This would typically be employed in cities with little available land and high land costs. By zoning exclusively for industrial uses, speculation-induced cost increases are minimized.

5. Height and density variances allow cities to waive certain restrictions in zoning ordinances. Developers may be allowed to exceed building height or density restrictions in exchange for providing some other benefit to the city such as low-cost housing.

6. Density transfers are similar to variances in that lower densities on one development site may be traded for higher densities on another.

7. It should be noted that the 29% may include training programs where the local government is acting as a broker for federal or provincial programs and may over represent the extent of municipal training initiatives.

8. Assisted housing is low-income housing, often provided by developers in return for height and density variances. Development is encouraged that would not have taken place under existing zoning ordinances, while still allowing the city to gain something in return.

9. It should be noted that the 2% here represents only one city in each case. A review of the survey forms indicated that different cities are using these prohibited techniques. In other words, it is not just one city engaging in all of the restricted incentives. There appears to be no pattern in the cities using financial incentives; they reflect a mix of size, economic stress, and so on.

REFERENCES

Albritton, R.B. and Brown, R. 1986. Intergovernmental impacts on policy variations within states: Effects of local discretion on general assistance programs. *Policy Studies Review* 5: 529-535.

Bingham, R.D. and Blair, J.P. 1984. Introduction: Urban economic development. In R.D. Bingham and J.P. Blair (eds.), *Urban economic development* (11-19) Urban Affairs Annual Reviews, 27. Beverly Hills: Sage Publications: 11-19.

Bucknall, B. 1988. Of deals and distrust: The perplexing perils of municipal bonusing. Paper prepared in 1988.

Dusenbury, P.J. 1980. *Suburbs in the city: Municipal boundary changes in the southern states*. Research Triangle Park, NC: The Southern Growth Policies Board.

Eisinger, P.K. 1988. *The rise of the entrepreneurial state*. Madison: University of Wisconsin Press.

Galloway, T.D. and Landis, J.D. 1986. How cities expand: Does state law make a difference? *Growth and Change* (October): 25-45.

Garber, J. and Imbroscio, D. 1989. Canadian federalism and economic development: The myth of the North American city reconsidered. Paper presented at the annual meeting of the American Political Science Association, Atlanta, GA.

Hill, R.C. 1984. Economic crisis and political response in the motor city. In L. Sawers and W.K. Tabb (eds.), *Sunbelt snowbelt urban development and regional restructuring* (pp. 313-338). New York/Oxford: Oxford University Press.

Jones, B.D. and Bachelor, L.W. 1984. Local policy discretion and the corporate surplus. In R.D. Bingham and J.P. Blair (eds.), *Urban economic development* (245-268). Urban Affairs Annual Reviews, 27. Beverly Hills: Sage Publications: 245-268.

Jones, B.D. and Vedlitz, A. 1988. Higher education policies and economic growth in the American states. *Economic Development Quarterly* 2 (February): 78-87.

Knight R.V. and Gappert G. 1984. Cities and the challenge of the global economy. In R.D. Bingham and J.P. Blair (eds.), *Urban economic development* (63-78). Urban Affairs Annual Reviews, 27. Beverly Hills: Sage Publications.

Matulef, M.L. 1987. Strategies for economic revitalization. Paper presented at the National Conference of the American Society for Public Administration, Boston, MA.

McManus, S.A. and Thomas, R.D. 1979. Expanding the tax base: Does annexation make a difference. *The Urban Interest* 1 (Fall): 15-28.

Pelissero, J.P. and Fasenfest, D. 1989. Suburban economic development policy. *Economic Development Quarterly* 3 (November): 301-311.

Peterson, P.E. 1981. *City limits*. Chicago: University of Chicago Press.

Reese, L.A. 1991. Municipal fiscal health and tax abatement policy. *Economic Development Quarterly* 5 (February): 23-32.

Reese, L.A. and Malmer, A.B. 1994. The effects of state enabling legislation on local economic development policies. *Urban Affairs Quarterly* 30 (September): 114-135.

Rubin, B.M. and Zorn, C.K. 1985. Sensible state and local economic development. *Public Administration Review* 45 (March/April): 333-340.

Sancton, A. and Montgomery, B. 1994. Municipal government and residential land development: A comparative study of London, Ontario, in the 1920's and 1980's. In F. Frisken (ed.), *The Changing Canadian metropolis: A public policy perspective* (777-798). Berkeley and Toronto: Institute of Governmental Studies Press/Canadian Urban Institute.

Stephens, G.R. 1974. State centralization and the erosion of local autonomy. *The Journal of Politics* 36 (February): 444-476.

Sternberg, E. 1987. A practitioner's classification of economic development policy instruments, with some inspiration from political economy. *Economic Development Quarterly* 1 (May): 149-161.

Stevens, J.M. and McGowan, R.P. 1987. Patterns and predictors of economic development power in local government: A policy perspective on issues in one state. *Policy Studies Review* 6 (February): 554-568.

Stonecash, J.M. 1985. Paths of fiscal centralization in the American states. *Policy Studies Journal* 13: 653-661.

Warner, P.D. 1987. Business climate, taxes, and economic development. *Economic Development Quarterly* 4 (November): 383-390.

Wassall, G. and Hellman, D. 1985. Financial incentives to industry and urban economic development. *Policy Studies Review* 4 (May): 626-640.

Wolkoff, M.J. 1992. Is economic development decision making rational? *Urban Affairs Quarterly* 27 (March): 340-355.

Wolman, H. 1993. Cross-national comparisons of urban economic programmes: Is policy transfer possible? In D. Fasenfest (ed.), *Community economic development* (14-42). London and New York: Macmillan/St. Martin's Press.

COMPARING ECONOMIC DEVELOPMENT POLICIES ACROSS THE BORDER[1]

The three previous chapters have posed and addressed several questions related to local economic development practices in Michigan and Ontario. To summarize, it appears that cities in the two nations are essentially similar in the types of strategies pursued. However, the more liberal state legislative environment in Michigan, allowing cities wide discretion in the use of financial incentives, appears to foster traditional supply-side or locational incentives. Provincial restrictions on financial bonuses in Ontario, on the other hand, appear to encourage more demand-oriented practices. The primary purpose of this chapter is to utilize the foregoing analyses to compare local economic development practices more explicitly. The objective is to determine whether--at least for economic development policy--cities in the two countries are significantly different, essentially similar, or converging, as much of the recent literature suggests.

Some variation can be expected, as the previous discussion suggests. First, it has been argued that Canadian cities have not experienced the level of economic and fiscal stress of many U.S. cities. Indeed, studies have indicated lower levels of manufacturing in Canada; thus local economic stress caused by declines in manufacturing employment should be mitigated. Smaller population loss in central cities also suggests less economic stress. Based on these factors, it is possible that Canadian cities will practice a similar variety of economic development techniques but to a lesser extent. In other words, lower levels of stress necessitate less local economic development activity.

Second, Canadian cities have less independence vis-à-vis provincial governments than cities in the U.S. Since many policy areas are controlled at the provincial level, it is reasonable to expect that more economic development policy activity is vested in the higher level of government. This, too, would suggest a more limited use of economic development incentives in Canadian cities.

Finally, the difference in enabling legislation allows for comparison of techniques used under very different regulatory environments. As noted previously, cities in Ontario are prohibited from using financial bonuses like loans and tax incentive schemes. Cities in Michigan, on the other hand, are allowed wide latitude in the types of incentives, particularly financial, they offer. Cities are authorized to use an industrial facilities tax for certain real and personal industrial property in lieu of the general ad valorem property tax. Such industrial tax abatements can be offered for periods of up to twelve years and can cover 100% of assessed value for a replacement facility and 50% for a new facility.

Thus, one can address the question of whether superior governmental restrictions on financial incentives cause cities to engage in a different mix of economic development techniques. Research on U.S. cities suggests that while state restrictions on financial incentives such as tax abatements do not cause a widespread shift toward demand-side policies, they do cause cities to reduce their use of tax incentives in general. Cities prohibited from abating appear to be fairly selective in their trade-offs, increasing the use of land-based incentives in general and some business creation techniques--shared equity in development projects, transfer of development rights, and technical assistance to new firms, in particular (Reese and Malmer, 1994).

Wolman (1993) has identified seven criteria upon which to base cross-national comparisons of economic development efforts. These criteria are used here to examine the impact of enabling legislation, economic stress, and other factors identified in the literature. Wolman's criteria include: structural environment, extent of problem condition, problem definition, policy objectives/goals, nature of resources brought to address problems, extent of resources employed, and impact of policies (1993, pgs. 17-18). This chapter focuses on these criteria, addressing several specific questions. Ideally, the comparison would also include the success of economic development policies, but the survey did not address that topic.

1) Do governmental and economic development organizational structures differ among cities in Ontario and Michigan? If so, what is the nature of these differences?
2) Does the extent of economic stress vary across cities?
3) Do cities exhibit similar goals and objectives for their economic development efforts?
4) Are there differences in resources allocated toward economic development?
5) Do cities implement different policies to foster economic development?

GOVERNMENTAL AND ORGANIZATIONAL STRUCTURE

Governmental structure was measured in several ways (see Table 5-1). First, local officials were asked about the structure of their local governments.[2] City elections in both nations are mostly nonpartisan; all Ontario cities have nonpartisan elections and all but a handful of cities in Michigan have nonpartisan elections. While Ontario cities generally have ward-based council elections (44%), elections in Michigan cities tend to be at-large (39%). Mayor systems predominate in Ontario (88%), while city managers are prevalent in Michigan (76%). The differences between chief executive and at-large versus ward elections are statistically significant at the .05 level.[3] From this analysis it would appear that local structural arrangements are more "reformed" in Michigan cities. Indeed, Michigan cities have a long tradition of "good government" with the typical "reforms"--nonpartisan and at-large elections and city managers--widespread within the state. Whether one can make substantive associations beyond this is open to question.

On the one hand, research has suggested that "reformed" systems should be less responsive to specialized group demands, particularly if the groups are geographically based (Lineberry and Fowler, 1967; Aiken, 1970; Karnig, 1975; Grimes et al., 1976; Heilig and Mundt, 1984; Meier and England, 1984; Svara, 1990; Polinard et al., 1994). However, other research has suggested that manager systems are also very responsive to group demands since the manager lacks an electoral constituency to secure his/her position (Greenstone and Peterson, 1968; Northrop and Dutton, 1978). Studies have also indicated that the impact of reformed structures varies depending upon the groups involved (Karnig, 1975). Still, more recent research suggests that unreformed structures have some interactive impact on minority access to public jobs (Mladenka, 1989), public sector salaries for minorities (Polinard et al., 1994), greater minority and low income representation on council (Welch and Bledsoe, 1988), more equitable educational policies (Meier and Stewart, 1991), and on program benefits to minority groups in general (Browning et al., 1984). Further, while Welch and Bledsoe (1988) found little difference in policy preferences among officials in unreformed and reformed cities, council members in the former were more likely to stress constituent services.

The whole issue may be moot for Ontario since most cities in Canada have not experienced a "reform" movement similar to that in the U.S., and governmental arrangements themselves have somewhat different meanings. For example, Canadian cities did not have the political party machines that developed in many U.S. cities--thus, "reforms" were not motivated by an attempt to weaken machine organizations (Quesnel, 1994). "Reforms" in Canadian cities were more directed at experimentation with new management structures such as the city administrator or commission and an effort to enhance democratic participation (Quesnel, 1994). Further, city managers or administrators in Canada may be less powerful generally than their counterparts in the U.S. Typically, city administrators or managers formulate policy, conduct day-to-day administrative duties, and prepare the budget in both nations. However, in Canadian cities, appointment and dismissal of department heads may only be "recommended" to council in many cases, thus making the position somewhat weaker than in the U.S. (Higgins, 1977).

Organizational arrangements for economic development are also significantly different. Ontario cities are more likely to have a free-standing department devoted solely to economic development (59%). Cities in Michigan are more likely to delegate economic development functions to another department such as community development (33%), or to fragment authority among several line departments (19%). External economic development commissions or corporations were more likely to be employed in Ontario (20%) than Michigan (2%).

As Stone's (1989) distinction between government and governing suggests, there is a difference between the formal organizational structures of a local government and the actual actors involved in "running" the city. Separate survey questions asked about influence in initiating economic development policy to get at this latter issue. In both countries, the most influential actor in promoting economic development was the city government. Beyond this, there is some divergence in actors identified as being active. For cities in Michigan, the next most important actors are a private sector body (19%) or a joint public/private organization (17%). In Ontario cities, public/private bodies were mentioned as being most influential more frequently than private sector bodies alone (13% and 8% respectively). Joint governmental bodies were also mentioned (8%).

While local officials in both nations indicated that the Economic Development Director was the lead actor in initiating economic development activities, this was more likely the case in Ontario. Respondents in Michigan also pointed to the mayor, city manager, business leaders, and "other" actors as being influential. None of these differences in locus of control or influence are statistically significant, however. Thus, while formal organizational arrangements are quite different, governing patterns in the two sets of cities are more similar.

THE EXTENT OF THE PROBLEM: ECONOMIC STRESS

Research suggests that while cities in Canada have not suffered the levels of economic stress and downturn present in many U.S. cities, municipalities in the two nations may be converging on this point. Since cities in Ontario contain significant levels of manufacturing employment, this may be more likely. Responses to a question concerning perception of economic base expansion or contraction over the past five years suggest that cities in Ontario have been significantly less stressed. However, it is important to note that the majority of officials in both nations indicated that at least some economic base expansion had occurred within their cities over the past five years (see Table 5-2).

ECONOMIC DEVELOPMENT GOALS

How officials defined the "problem" of economic development was gauged by asking officials about priorities from a list of 11 possible economic development goals. City officials in both countries identified similar economic development goals. Indeed four of the five top goals are identical; attraction of new business, retention of existing business, economic base diversification, and industrial development (see Table 5-3). The cities differ significantly on only four of the 11 goals; business attraction, downtown development, economic base diversification, and tourism. Ontario officials are significantly more likely to indicate that diversification, business attraction, and tourism were important goals. Michigan officials, on the other hand, were significantly more likely to stress downtown development.

RESOURCES

The survey asked respondents to indicate the number of staff devoted primarily or solely to economic development activities and the percentage of time the person responsible for economic development worked specifically on economic development activities. According to these indicators, Ontario cities devote significantly greater resources to economic development. Cities in Ontario are most likely to have three persons working in economic development, and the person responsible for that area spends 87% of his/her time directly on economic development. For Michigan cities the modal personnel allocation is actually zero, and the director or other actor mainly responsible for economic development devotes only 55% of his/her time to that effort. The specific question asked was how many staff, including the economic development director, worked solely or primarily on economic development activities. Clearly, in Michigan, most of the personnel working on economic development in fact spend the majority of their time on other activities.

ECONOMIC DEVELOPMENT ACTIVITIES

Respondents were asked about the extent to which they rely on over 50 economic development mechanisms or strategies divided into five policy categories; governmental regulations, public infrastructure investment, financial incentives, land and property management, and marketing activities. Of the activities listed, cities in the two nations differed significantly on 26, with most of the variation in the promotional and financial categories. Cities in Ontario rely much more heavily on marketing or promotional activities than do those in Michigan (see Table 5-4). Indeed, they are significantly more likely to employ 10 of the 11 mechanisms in the category. The two sets of cities are similar only in their efforts to promote specific development sites.

Just the opposite pattern occurs for financial incentives. Cities in Michigan are significantly more likely to use five of the 11 incentives listed in the survey. Cities in the two nations are similar in their propensity to use deferred tax payments, enterprise zones, offer in-kind services, business incubators, and sale-lease back arrangements. In these cases few if any cities in either country employ such mechanisms. More frequently used techniques in this category for Ontario cities are worker training programs (29%), while Michigan cities are most likely to offer tax abatements (83%), and development bonds (39%). Ontario cities are significantly more likely to use only one financial technique--worker training programs.

It should be noted, however, that even given the greater reliance on marketing mechanisms in Ontario, cities in both nations rely heavily on promotional activities to foster economic development. Indeed, when average usage rates are calculated by category, marketing mechanisms rank first for Ontario cities and second for Michigan cities. For both groups of cities promotional brochures, inventories of development sites, site promotion, and visits to prospects rank among the most heavily used techniques.

Cities in both nations also tend to rely heavily on infrastructure improvements to foster economic development. Indeed, this category ranks second for cities in Ontario and first for cities in Michigan in overall usage. Many cities in both nations improve pedestrian amenities, parking, traffic circulation and streets, improve the visual presentation of their communities, and engage in historic preservation. However, cities in Ontario are significantly more likely to engage in four activities in this area; improvement of recreation services and facilities, creation/improvement of water and sewage systems, and the designation of community improvement areas.

Overall, the category of governmental regulations ranks third for Ontario cities and fourth for Michigan cities; the cities are significantly different in their use of only three of the 10 techniques in the category. Cities in Ontario are significantly more likely to regulate facades and impose design requirements on industrial parks. Cities in Michigan are significantly more likely to have historic district regulations. Overall, cities in both nations are most likely to ease building inspection procedures to facilitate development and regulate the use of signs to improve community appearance.

Cities in Ontario and Michigan are almost identical in their reliance on land and property management techniques. Indeed, the cities were significantly different on only three of the 12 techniques in the category. Cities in Ontario are more likely to operate municipal industrial parks while cities in Michigan are more likely to rehabilitate older buildings for developmental use and clear land of unusable structures. Cities in both nations tend to rely most heavily on the purchase and sale of land for development.

COMPARING ECONOMIC DEVELOPMENT PRACTICES

What can be concluded in using Wolman's criteria for cross-national comparison? Are policies essentially similar and, if so, are they produced by the same forces? This analysis suggests that, for economic development policy, cities in Canada and the U.S. are remarkably similar. It can be argued that this is the case because local economic development policies are driven by essentially the same forces in the post-industrial world; international business fluctuations, competition between nations and hence cities for development, and transportation and communication changes allowing for separation of production and management functions and markets. Similar forces give rise to similar policies among cities in different nations. Differences, particularly in policy mechanisms, tend to be in scale, with some limited affects resulting from governmental and legislative framework and possibly social history.

While Ontario and Michigan cities differ in local governmental structure and the organization of economic development functions, governing arrangements are very similar, reflecting the role of local government officials and, more particularly, economic development professionals.

The extent of the problem of economic stress appears to be more severe among Michigan cities. However, in both cases, local officials almost overwhelmingly perceive that there has been at least some growth in the local economy. Differences, again, appear to be of scale; officials in both countries perceive a growing economy, but the tendency is stronger in Ontario. As noted previously, the difference also stems primarily from a few Ontario officials indicating strong declines in their economic base. A more interesting question is raised here, however. If local officials appear to perceive economic growth in their localities, what forces are driving the "arms race" nature of local economic development? The role of competition with other cities and the professional values and political environment of economic development personnel clearly require closer examination.

While cities in Ontario devote significantly more resources to economic development, officials in both nations appear to be quite uniform in defining the problem. Top economic development goals are identical across the two sets of cities; retention and attraction of investment, and economic base diversification with a continued stress on industry. The variation in resource allocation could result from several sources: 1) a decision by Ontario cities to devote greater effort toward economic development, suggesting a higher priority for this function overall; 2) the existence of greater economic growth or at least less decline among Ontario cities, thus making more resources available for economic development activities; or 3) greater professionalization of the economic development function among cities in Ontario.

There is some evidence to support the latter contention. First, the longer history of planning noted in the Canadian literature opens doors for influence by trained professionals. Further, the presence of a free-standing economic development department headed by its own director, the greater perceived influence of economic development directors, and more staff and staff time devoted to economic development, all suggest higher levels of professionalism. This issue, too, needs to be addressed more explicitly.

The specific mechanisms employed to foster economic development are generally similar with few differences. An examination of general trends and priorities clearly suggests that economic development policy is essentially comparable in the two nations. Public infrastructure investment and marketing activities predominate while financial strategies as a whole are less widely employed. In almost all cases the same techniques predominate in both nations. The differences present tend to be of scale not content. Indeed, of the top ten techniques used in each nation, seven are the same (see Table 5-5).[4]

There are some differences in policies employed, however. At the outset it was expected that Canadian cities would exhibit a lower level of economic development policy activity. However, cities in Ontario are more likely to practice economic development techniques in three of the five categories; governmental regulation, infrastructure investment, and promotion. This may stem from the greater resource commitment, having more resources available, or to historic and cultural variations in acceptance of government intervention in the private sector. Thus, cities in Canada may intervene to a greater extent in business development due to a past history of acceptance of such intervention. As Bartik suggests,

> In the United States, such government intervention with individual businesses is viewed with suspicion by both liberals and conservatives. Conservatives worry about excessive government interference with the market; liberals worry about government subsidies to wealthy business owners (1991, 100).

It also appears that provincial restrictions on financial incentives reduce the reliance on such techniques, and concomitantly, increase the use of other types of strategies. For Ontario cities it is clear that marketing activities and infrastructure investment are predominant. However, land based techniques like land acquisition and industrial parks are important as well. The overall picture is somewhat different for Michigan cities, where several financial and land-based strategies predominate.

In light of earlier discussions, it appears that supra-government limitations on financial incentives can affect local economic development policy choices. While Chapter 3 noted a continuing reliance on supply-side activities in Michigan cities, Chapter 4 showed that cities in Ontario utilize more demand-side activities. This contrast is clearly visible in the direct comparison. Cities in Ontario employ the following techniques at higher rates; employee training programs, business incubators, industrial property management, development of export markets, and market development planning. Differences for training, export marketing, and development planning are significant. However, a final caveat is in order here. On the whole, demand-side activities are not widely practiced by cities in either nation. Market development planning and export market development are the only demand-side strategies employed by a majority of cities.

For cities in Ontario and Michigan, it appears that comparisons of local economic development are feasible and instructive. The differences in the use of specific techniques notwithstanding, it is clear that basic commonalties exist between economic development policies. With the exception of some financial incentives, the spectrum of strategies employed is remarkably uniform. The main difference between Michigan and Ontario cities revolves around financial incentives and appears to be a function of supra-government enabling legislation rather than any systematic variance between cities in the two countries.

The preceding description and comparison of local economic development policy in Ontario and Michigan cities suggests several conclusions:

1) Cities in both nations pursue a remarkably similar mix of economic development strategies.
2) Provincial restrictions on financial bonuses reduce the use of such incentives in Ontario cities.
3) As a result, Ontario cities are somewhat more likely to use certain demand-side incentives.

4) However, the use of demand-side incentives is quite low among cities in both nations.

Other researchers have argued that the increasing convergence in economic development policy among cities in the U.S. and Canada is the result of similar external economic forces. The discussion here also raises questions about the effects of other factors; intercity competition, the perceptions of local economic development officials, the extent of resources devoted to economic development, and the level of professionalism in the local economic development organization. In light of the basic similarity in economic development policy in U.S. and Canadian cities, it can be posited that "nation of origin" is not determinantly important in local policy. Given this, what "other" factors might affect local development policy? The goal of the following chapters is to provide a better understanding of the forces which lead cities to employ the types and mix of strategies they do.

TABLE 5-1
Organizational Structure

	Ontario	Michigan
Economic Development*		
Located in executive office	05%	17%
Centralized in a separate department	59%	15%
Decentralized among line departments	02%	19%
Part of a larger department	07%	33%
External commission/corporation	20%	02%
Other	07%	02%
Governing System		
Most active in promoting economic development:		
city	68%	55%
public/private body	13%	17%
joint government	08%	06%
private sector body	08%	19%
Most influential actor:		
city manager	05%	15%
mayor	10%	17%
economic development director	71%	28%
economic development commissioner	07%	09%
business leaders	02%	13%
other	05%	17%

* Values are significantly different at the .05 level.

TABLE 5-2
Economic Stress

Economic Base*	Ontario	Michigan
Rapid expansion	29%	09%
Moderate growth	33%	35%
Slow growth	26%	30%
Stability	07%	11%
Modest decline	05%	11%
Significant decline	00%	04%

* Percentages are significantly different at the .05 level.

TABLE 5-3
Economic Development Goals

	Mean Priority Ranking**	
	Ontario	Michigan
Base diversification*	2.30	2.96
Attraction*	1.95	2.69
Retention	2.29	2.24
Minority business	4.37	4.11
Downtown development*	3.63	2.68
Neighborhood development	4.16	3.76
Small business	3.42	3.47
Tourism*	3.59	4.11
Service sector	3.80	3.93
Corporate headquarters	3.79	3.59
Industrial development	2.64	2.55

* Percentages are significantly different at the .05 level.
** Lower score indicates higher priority

TABLE 5-4
Economic Development Policies

Mechanisms	Percent Using the Technique	
	Ontario	Michigan
Government Regulations		
One-stop permits	21	17
Eased building inspection	55	63
Ombudsperson	21	30
Eased zoning process	36	35
Relaxed environmental regs.	00	02
Historic district regs.*	12	32
Sign regulations	60	48
Facade regulations*	38	15
Anti-litter regs.	19	07
Industrial park design regs.*	79	22
Infrastructure Investments		
Parking	67	65
Streets	76	61
Sanitation	38	37
Pedestrian amenities	79	63
Beautification	74	65
Recreation*	88	61
Historic preservation	33	19
Sewage*	64	43
Water*	57	35
Community improvement areas*	60	03
Financial Incentives		
Tax abatements*	00	83
Deferred taxes	02	11
Enterprise zones	00	07
In-kind services	05	17
Employee training*	29	11
Direct loans*	02	28
Loan guarantees*	07	24
Loan subsidies*	02	28
Incubators	26	19
Sale-lease back	10	11
Development bonds	00	39

Table 5-4 (continued)

Land and Property Management

Lot consolidation	38	41
Land expropriation	17	06
Land purchase	81	63
Business relocation	19	19
Site development*	17	54
Sale of land to developers	62	70
Donation of land	05	11
Leasing of land	14	19
Office/retail property management	00	07
Industrial property management	24	15
Rehabilitation of buildings*	05	39
Industrial parks*	86	39

Marketing Activities

Business liaison committees*	67	44
Inventory of sites	93	83
Promotional literature*	100	70
Videos*	79	26
Solicit foreign business*	93	26
Visits to prospects*	95	52
Trade shows*	98	32
Develop export markets*	57	15
Site promotion*	74	52
Special events*	60	24
Market develop. pln.*	55	28

* Percentages are significantly different at the .05 level.

TABLE 5-5
Top Ten Techniques

Ontario	Michigan
Promotional literature	Tax abatements/inventory of sites
Trade shows	Sale of land/promotional literature
Visits to prospects	Parking/pedestrian amenities
Foreign business attraction/ inventory of sites	Streamlined building insp.
Recreation services	Street improvements/ recreation services
Industrial parks	Visits to prospects/site promotion
Land purchase	Sign regulations
Videos/industrial park design requirements/pedestrian amenities	Liaison committees
Street improvements	Sewage system improvements
Site promotion/beautification	

NOTES

1. Some earlier data analysis from this chapter was published as Local Economic Development Across the Northern Border, *Urban Affairs Quarterly*, 28 (June 1993): 571-592.

2. Some of the indicators of structure are problematic due to question composition on the survey. Since respondents were asked about various elements of structure such as at-large elections, partisan elections, and the presence of a city manager, using individual questions, percentages do not necessarily add to 100 in each case.

3. Significant differences are based on bivariate correlations of nation and the variable of interest.

4. While Table 5 presents the top ten mechanisms for each set of cities, 14-15 different techniques are included in each due to ties in ranking. Thus, the comparison is really seven out of this higher number.

REFERENCES

Aiken, M. 1970. The distribution of community power: Structural bases and social consequences. In M. Aiken and P. Mott (eds.), *The structure of community power* (487-525). New York: Random House.

Browning, R.P., Marshall, D.R. and Tabb, D.H. 1984. *Protest is not enough.* Berkeley: University of California Press.

Greenstone, J.D. and Peterson, P.E. 1968. Reformers, machines and the war on poverty. In J.Q. Wilson (ed.), *City politics and public policy* (pp. 267-292). New York: John Wiley.

Grimes, M.D., Bonjean, C.M., Lyon, J.L. and Lineberry, R.L. 1976. Community structure and leadership arrangements: A multidimensional analysis. *American Sociological Review* 41 (August): 706-725.

Heilig, P. and Mundt, R.J. 1984. *Your voice at city hall: The politics and policies of district representation.* Albany: State University of New York Press.

Higgins, D.L. 1977. *Urban Canada government and politics.* Toronto: Macmillan Canada.

Karnig, A.K. 1975. Private-regarding policy, civil rights groups, and the mediating impact of municipal reforms. *American Journal of Political Science* 19 (February): 91-106.

Lineberry, R.L. and Fowler, E.P. 1967. Reformism and public policies in American cities. *American Political Science Review* 61 (September): 701-716.

Meier, K.J. and England, R.E. 1984. Black representation and educational policy: Are they related? *American Political Science Review* 78: 392-403.

Meier, K.J. and Stewart, J. 1991. *The politics of hispanic education.* Albany: State University of New York Press.

Mladenka, K.P. 1989. Blacks and Hispanics in urban politics. *American Political Science Review* 83 (March): 165-191.

Northrop, A. and Dutton, N. 1978. Municipal reform and group influence. *American Journal of Political Science* 22 (August): 691-711.

Polinard, J.L., Wrinkle, R.D., Longoria, T. and Binder, N.E. 1994. *Electoral structure and urban policy.* New York: ME Sharpe.

Quesnel, L. 1994. Part politics in the metropolis: Montreal 1960-1990. In F. Frisken (ed.), *The changing Canadian metropolis: A public policy perspective* (581-612). Berkeley: Institute of Governmental Studies Press and Toronto: Canadian Urban Institute.

Reese, L.A. and Malmer, A.B. 1994. The effects of state enabling legislation on local economic development policies. *Urban Affairs Quarterly* 30 (September): 114-135.

Stone, C. 1989. *Regime politics: Governing Atlanta.* Lawrence: University Press of Kansas.

Svara, J.H. 1990. *Official leadership in the city.* Oxford: Oxford University Press.

76

Welch, S. and Bledsoe, T. 1988. *Urban reform and its consequences a study in representation*. Chicago: University of Chicago Press.

Wolman, H. 1993. Cross-national comparisons of urban economic programmes: Is policy transfer possible? In D. Fasenfest (ed.), *Community economic development: Policy formation in the U.S. and U.K.* (14-42). London: Macmillan and New York: St. Martin's Press.

CHAPTER 6

EXPLAINING LOCAL ECONOMIC DEVELOPMENT POLICIES[1]

The forgoing chapters have described and compared economic development practices in cities in Ontario and Michigan. The task remaining is to explain why cities engage in the activities they do. This chapter examines various explanations or determinants of economic development policy, assesses the shortcomings and limitations of these efforts, and offers some additional thoughts about policy processes in local governments. The ultimate goal is to create a more complete model explaining economic development policy outcomes. Such a model is then tested in succeeding chapters.

THE DETERMINANTS OF ECONOMIC DEVELOPMENT POLICY

The literature on why certain cities engage in certain types of economic development techniques tends to be fragmented and contradictory. It focuses on only a few independent variables at a time and rests primarily on data from U.S. cities. Factors such as age of municipality and governmental structure have been found to both increase and decrease the use of various economic development incentives (Fernandez and Pincus, 1982; Levy, 1981; Pelissero, 1986). For other variables--median income, property value, local tax rate, the amount of professionalism in the economic development function--reasonable arguments can be made for affects in opposite directions.

An emerging body of research suggests that more prosperous cities use economic development incentives to a greater degree than less prosperous cities. Such a finding is counterintuitive on its face since healthy and growing communities do not need to offer incentives. But, it appears they use their greater financial ability to promote even further growth. Further, research has indicated that firms tend to locate in areas that are already economically successful, thus allowing cities to prosper without incentives. It is also likely that firms will seek incentives from attractive cities (Schneider, 1986; Rubin, 1988). Indeed, state-level research has indicated that healthier areas are more likely to grant tax abatements (Brierly, 1986), and research on Michigan communities found that more fiscally sound cities offered higher levels of tax abatements (Reese, 1991). Still, other authors have found the reverse to be true; cities experiencing high levels of economic stress may be driven to offer incentives to improve their economic position (Rubin and Rubin, 1987; Reese, 1992).

Recent research on economic development in the U.S. also suggests that cities with more professionalized economic development programs engage in more economic development efforts (Pelissero and Fasenfest, 1989; Reese, 1991). Research on U.S. cities also indicates that competition from nearby municipalities results in increased use of development incentives (Bingham, 1976; Pelissero, 1986; Bowman, 1988). Given the information imbalance facing cities, unsure of what is necessary to attract firms, municipalities are driven to offer all possible inducements (Jones and Bachelor, 1984). This is exacerbated when cities know that others are waiting in the wings competing for the same firms.

Governmental structure appears to play a role in economic development practices. But, the findings suggest that cities with both "reformed" and "unreformed" structures are more predisposed to offer economic development incentives (among others see Lineberry and Fowler, 1967; Karnig, 1975; Northrop and Dutton, 1978; Feiock, 1989; Rosenfeld et al., 1995).

Other variables also seem to affect local economic development policy. Growing populations appear to attract business, perhaps due to greater perceived opportunities for sales and skilled employees, among other reasons (Kieschnick, 1981; Schneider, 1986). Location and proximity to other competing cities has been found to affect both the creation of enterprise zones (Green and Brintnall, 1986) and use of tax incentives (Bingham, 1976; Levy, 1981; Pelissero, 1986; Bowman, 1988). Age of a community seems important, with newer cities more receptive to economic development activities (Levy, 1981), and older and younger cities more aggressive in their economic development strategies (Pelissero, 1986).

Regarding more "political" variables, citizen pressure or expectations may increase the level of local economic development policy activity. Rubin and Zorn (1985) suggest that citizens expect local officials to enact policies which further economic development, and political attitudes toward business appear to be important as well (Schmenner, 1982; Goldstein, 1985).

Such findings provide interesting insights into the economic development policy process. They fail in a collective sense to provide a theoretically cohesive explanation of policy outcomes, however, because they lack explicit attention to broader issues of agency and control. In short, focusing on individual "determinants" represents a piecemeal attempt to explain local policy choices. And, most research has ignored several fundamental questions: who controls such decisions? what are the relative impacts of external forces and internal actions? and, how are decisions actually made?

URBAN DEPENDENCY VERSUS LOCAL POLITICS

A central debate in the local economic development literature has revolved around whether independent actions by local officials can be influential, given the very real economic constraints they face. In short, the question is one of dependency versus local political agency. This serves as the starting point for a more comprehensive explanation of local economic development policy-making.

While many authors have made the argument that economic development policy is largely determined by outside forces, Peterson (1981) has presented the most complete discussion. He views cities as having one consistent "interest," that of preserving and furthering their economic position. This interest is determined by the fixed location of cities and uncontrollable structural economic factors. Since cities can not control larger economic forces, the movement of labor and capital for example, and because they are in competition with others, "developmental policies," those which enhance the local economic position, will be primary. In short,

> A great deal can be said about local public policy without considering any variations in the recruitment of elected officials, the strength of political parties, the degree of organized group activity, or the level of turnout in local elections. Power forces external to the city carry great weight in local policy-making (Peterson, 1981, p. 64).

Recent empirical research has supported this view (Longoria, 1994). Beaumont and Hovey state simply that "much of what happens in the American economy, and thus the economies of states and communities, is totally beyond the control of state and local governments" (1985, p. 330). Many concur that cities today are intricately linked to external systems; state and national governments, the larger national economy, national and multinational firms, other cities and regions, financial institutions and even international markets and other countries (Katznelson, 1976; Molotch and Logan, 1985; Kantor, 1987, among others).

While it does seem clear that external economic and political forces strongly affect local governments, still at issue is the question of whether cities have any room to maneuver within these constraints. Is all economic development policy determined by a unified city interest as Peterson suggests? Are local politics of little or no importance? Other authors strongly disagree that this is the case.

Jones and Bachelor (1986, p. 212) take a middle ground, suggesting that cities have the ability to make "creative bounded choice." In other words, while they are constrained by external forces, local officials do have room to make decisions and "exploit weaknesses in the environment." Thus, they argue that while business or economic interests do not totally control cities, they do serve as a "sustaining hand." Specifically "...the giant industrial companies do provide the backdrop against which the public-policy process operates in the industrial city. They are always there, seldom intervening in specific policy matters but never far from the calculations of policy makers" (Jones and Bachelor, 1986, p. 216).

Stone (1987) goes even further and suggests greater local independence in economic development policy decisions. While he acknowledges that constraints or "structural boundaries" are present, he sees opportunities for

81

independent action. Local decision makers do not simply follow the imperatives that emanate from the national political economy; they must interpret those imperatives, apply them to local conditions, and act on them within the constraints of the political arrangements they build and maintain. In short, "...urban politics still matters" (Stone, 1987, p. 4).

Unlike Peterson, Stone argues that there is no single urban interest. Rather, conflicts often arise regarding economic development policy, and there are definite winners and losers. Recent articles on local support for no-growth policies attest to the view that no singular city interest drives economic development policy (Logan and Molotch, 1987; Vogel and Swanson, 1989; Bollens, 1990).

It seems quite reasonable then to acknowledge that local political arrangements are important and that local officials can affect the economic situation within very real external constraints. As Stone states, local officials "...are the architects of their own responses to the structural constraints and changing conditions in which city politics is embedded" (Stone, 1987, p. 14).

Once it is agreed that local politics does matter, still left to debate is the type of independent decision-making employed. If local economic development decisions can have an impact, then it becomes vital to understand the nature of those decisions.

THE NATURE OF LOCAL ECONOMIC DEVELOPMENT DECISIONS

Some authors have suggested that local economic decisions are based on rational analysis. While agreeing that politics does matter "...in the direction, duration, and development of urban space," Pagano and Bowman suggest that economic development policy decisions are largely the result of a fairly rational analysis of risks and possible costs and benefits to the city (1989, p. 1). They do not go so far as to suggest that urban economic development decision-making is rational in a strict "revenue-maximizing" sense. However, they see it as being "purposive and deliberate." Decisions are based on an examination of the city's position among other cities, the aspirations of local officials regarding future positions, and achievement of balance between tax and service levels. In short, "development incentives offered by cities are never projects undertaken blindly or lightly" (Pagano and Bowman, 1989, p. 6). While not fully the rational model of decision-making described by Wildavsky (1979) and others, Pagano and Bowman suggest that cities identify certain goals and weigh policies against the achievement of those goals. In short, the role of public officials "is to define their vision for the city" and "to identify the public economic development tools to accomplish that vision, and to decide the extent of city intervention in the process" (Pagano and Bowman, 1995, p. 3).

Other authors have questioned the extent of rationality evidenced in local economic development decision-making. As Stone states: "...any policy, no matter how sincerely put forward as being in the public interest, is inescapably shaped by those who carry it out; it is shaped by their interests, their perceptions, their mode of operation, and their particular form of interdependence with one another" (Stone, 1987, p. 11). Thus, those that carry out economic development policy, however rationally intended, also strongly mold it. Jones and Bachelor agree, noting that:

> It would be a mistake, however, to characterize economic-development policies as being solely "rational and efficient." While there certainly exists an element of rational analysis in this policy arena, there is also a considerable amount of political conflict, of negotiating among interests, of symbolic appeal, of incomplete information, and of snap decisions (1986, p. 200).

It can reasonably be argued then that economic development policies are not wholly rational and are strongly influenced by implementing officials. Economic development policy is likely to be more heavily shaped by the implementation process and the implementors themselves than by any rational or systematic decisions on the part of local officials. Indeed, Meyer concludes that in economic development policy-making:

> Decision-makers' personal characteristics appeared to carry more weight in shaping economic development strategies than did their economic motivations. Economics, education and work experience in economic development clearly induced more conservative policy orientations on the part of our respondents. This claim for a dominant role for indoctrination and values inculcation as molders of strategic choices is bolstered by our findings (1993, pg. 138).

Rubin (1990) has explicitly examined the role of economic development professionals in the policy process. Initial research suggested that officials tried everything they were familiar with or what others were doing in the hopes that something would promote development (Rubin, 1988). Further research, however, indicates greater complexity. It appears that economic development officials who feel that they have little control over their environment tend to engage in more formal activities which have little direct relationship to economic development goals. Rubin notes:

> ...in municipalities that consider economic development less controllable and perceive that cities are in a zero-sum competition for businesses there is a tendency to tackle symbolic showcase projects or formalistic "make work" efforts, rather than expend efforts on less glamorous, but ultimately more productive, economic development activities (Rubin, 1990. p. 114).

Other authors agree that bureaucratic actions affect economic development outcomes. Indeed, Schneider quotes Blair, et al., who state that the economic development arena has

> ...created a powerful bureaucratic structure with the specific mission of encouraging economic development. These bureaucrats may pursue deals to justify their jobs and their salaries, without judging the more general societal payoffs of their actions (Schneider, 1989, p. 32).

It appears, then, that local politics and decisions do matter in economic development, within certain constraints. Further, these local decisions appear to be driven less by rational or systematic analysis than actions of economic development professionals. Thus, the role of bureaucrats must be explored more fully.

BUREAUCRATIC DECISION RULES

The central thesis presented here is that economic development policy-making tends to be heavily influenced by bureaucratic or professional actors and is based more on decision rules or procedures than rational analysis. The logic of this argument rests on a significant amount of research on bureaucratic decision rules. Such rules or standard operating procedures have been found to affect many policy areas, from foreign policy (Allison, 1971) to urban service delivery (Jones, et al., 1980). As Jones and his colleagues state, "the influence of service rules indicates the necessity of studying the internal structures and processes of service bureaucracies in attempting to understand local public policy" (1980, p. 246). Specifically, decision rules are the "routinized procedures for accomplishing the purpose of the organization" (Jones, et al., 1980, p. 228). They are used by bureaucrats to simplify decision-making, are influenced by professional standards, and tend to reduce uncertainty and encourage coordination. In urban service distribution, for example, bureaucratic decisions influence "who gets what" amount of local service. Decision rules in this case are based on professional standards, often stressing efficiency in the delivery of services. While intended to be "neutral," decision rules have been shown to have equity impacts (Jones, et al., 1980, among others).

The notion that decision rules reduce uncertainty for bureaucrats is an important one. Lipsky (1980) probably best documents the environment of many bureaucrats in his book on street level bureaucracy. Bureaucrats that deal directly with the public tend to operate in an environment which is uncertain and often hostile, with goals that are changing, competing, or unclear. As a result, they rely on coping techniques or decision rules which serve to simplify the situation. These include changing perceptions of clients, displacing goals with what really can be achieved, and relying on standard operating procedures. Thus, decision rules are a classic formula for dealing with environmental stress.

While the street level literature focuses on low level bureaucrats, economic development officials share many of the same characteristics. Because economic development departments are often small--the director may be the only employee--department heads often deal directly with the public (Reese, 1993). Further, the environment of economic development professionals is uncertain. Rubin (1990, p. 113) found that professionals complained "that they lacked the ability to control economic factors yet were expected to produce results." They must deal with "environmental uncertainty," and with citizens and elected officials who do not understand the job and set conflicting and unclear goals. Thus, although they operate at a higher organizational level, economic development professionals experience conditions similar to street level bureaucrats and they are likely to exhibit similar coping techniques.

Part of this argument rests on the additional assumption that many decisions made by economic development directors are routine. Some authors have tended to assume that economic development policies are not routine-- they tend to be costly, often involving major investment or infrastructure development (McGowan and Stevens, 1983; Rubin, 1990). Others have noted that many aspects of economic development are routinized. For example, Jones and Bachelor (1986, p. 205) note that "economic development is a prime candidate for peak bargaining, but only when major projects are contemplated. (Much of policy making in the economic-development sphere is as routinized as it is in other areas of policy.)" Indeed, the analysis presented in Chapter 5 supports this argument. An examination of the top ten economic development techniques indicates that the majority are indeed fairly small scale and routine; promotional literature, trade shows, site promotion, city beautification, sign regulations, inventories of sites, visits to prospective firms, and liaison committees.

Thus, much of what economic development directors do is clearly routine; major projects which require a redirection of resources and garner the limelight are few and far between. The bottom line is that economic development policies tend to be driven by routinized decision rules which:

- are employed widely among the people making decisions and tend to limit discussion to just a few alternatives,
- serve to simplify decisions in a turbulent environment, and
- foster political stability both for the organization and the professionals involved (Sharkansky, 1970).

THE BUREAUCRATIC EXPLANATION

In summary, it appears clear that the determinants research to date is problematic in that it offers contradictory findings based on variation in data collected, operationalization (definition) of indicators, mix of variables examined, statistical technique employed, and sample analyzed. Further, various models explain widely varying amounts of policy behavior; Green and Fleischmann (1991) accounted for .159 to .285 of the variance in economic development activities, while research by Reese (1991, 1992) accounted for .39 to .89 of the variance in policy choices respectively. Such variation has much to do with differences in measurement and operationalization as well as explanatory variables.

The shortcomings in current models used to "explain" economic development policies result from several factors; failure to include the impact of bureaucrats in the process, insufficient attention to the procedures and criteria used to make decisions, lack of attention to the interplay between the environment and such decision-making criteria, and the absence of important variables. To more fully explain economic development outcomes, models must include a variety of important factors; structural, fiscal, political, bureaucratic, and procedural. Such a model is presented and tested in the next chapter. Prior to that, the validity of the bureaucratic explanation must be established.

SOME PROPOSITIONS ON THE BUREAUCRATIC ROLE

While the literature supports the importance of a variety of variables from age of municipality to the competitiveness of elections, the bureaucratic connections remain insufficiently explored in the context of economic development policy. To include the role of bureaucracy as a reasonable part of a model explaining economic development policy outcomes, the following propositions must be supported:

- Economic development decisions are largely left to economic development professionals in bureaucratic agencies.
- The environment for economic development decision-making is perceived as turbulent and uncertain.
- Policy decisions made by economic development professionals are based on decision rules or simplifying procedures.
- Decision rules tend not to be based on rational or systematic analysis of costs and benefits or other analytic approaches.

These propositions have been operationalized and explored in the manner described below. To develop an explanatory theory, the Ontario and Michigan responses have been combined into a single data set. The analysis in Chapter 5 clearly suggests that the two groups of cities are sufficiently similar in their economic development practices to warrant such combined analysis. Further, the remaining goal is the creation of a theory of economic development policy which applies cross-nationally. Any important differences between the Ontario and Michigan cities will be noted as the analysis proceeds.

* *Economic development decisions are largely left to economic development professionals.*

The extent of decision-making left to economic development professionals is examined using responses to questions regarding power and locus of decision-making from economic development directors, city managers, and mayors. This also includes whether economic development decisions are initiated or made by economic development professionals or city council, whether they are primarily driven by the professional training of bureaucrats, and whether citizens have any input.

* *The environment for economic development decision-making is turbulent and uncertain.*

The amount of stress economic development officials experience will be directly related to the amount of turmoil in their environment. Measures of "environmental turbulence" were developed based on analysis by Rubin (1990). They measure the extent to which officials believe that they can not control the future, that no one understands the problems they face, and that businesses play the city off against others in investment decisions. Presence of such perceptions are likely to indicate greater stress, leading to use of decision rules to simplify, regularize, and control the environment.

* *Policy decisions made by economic development professionals are based on decision rules or simplifying procedures.*

Operationalizing decision rules is complicated and relies on a variety of measures. Many authors have identified various decision procedures used by economic development bureaucrats. In examining the relationship between environmental stress and the behavior of economic development officials, Rubin (1990) found that increasing turbulence caused officials to increase the amount of formalistic or symbolic activity. Indeed, Stone (1987) suggests that officials often "substitute show for substance" in economic development. In a similar vein, Doig (1987) feels that officials are pressured to have "visible successes."

Wolman (1988), in explaining why local policy-makers continued to offer incentives such as tax abatements in the face of considerable academic literature disputing their effectiveness, identified several decision rules. First, officials will use incentives if they have little or no cost to the municipality. Second, incentives are used because they are a visible and symbolic effort that causes citizens and businesses to feel that something is being done. Finally, since it is still unclear whether incentives work, it is better to gamble that they do than to avoid them and have them work for neighboring cities.

Finally, Levenbach (1986) highlights seven decision rules used in the federal Economic Development Administration. They include tendencies to respond to external problems rather than being proactive, and filtering out undesirable proposals before they have to be considered fully, often by supplying misinformation. Such techniques tend to reduce uncertainty and stress in evaluating economic development projects.

Two sets of questions were identified for this research. Although the questions are similar to those used by Rubin (1990), they have been separated into two groups representing different types of rules. Based on Rubin's findings that economic development directors "shoot anything that flies" in their uncertainty over which techniques work, one set measures the tendency to use all types of economic development incentives permitted by the state/province or demanded by business. The second set measures another decision rule, goal displacement, pursuing symbol over substance in an effort to reduce uncertainty over what is expected.

* *Decision rules tend not to be based on rational or systematic analysis.*

The extent of rational decision-making is measured using several questionnaire items. According to many authors, rationality in policy-making involves having unified, consistent goals; trying to achieve objectives at the lowest cost; identifying all possible alternative solutions; evaluating alternatives in a systematic fashion; selecting and implementing a solution; and evaluating the ultimate effectiveness/efficiency of the policy solution (Churchman, 1969; Wildavsky, 1979). For purposes of this research, rational decision-making is measured by the presence of an economic development plan identifying goals, the use of some systematic procedure for evaluating alternatives--for example, cost/benefit analysis, linear programming or even regularized city council review--and evaluation of policies after implementation. Thus, questions address the extent of planning which takes place prior to program implementation and the amount of post hoc evaluation.

The following analysis suggests substantial bureaucratic involvement in the economic development decision-making process and significant reliance on decision rules in that process. To increase the number of cases and identify general trends the analysis uses the combined data set (N = 95 cities) in most cases. Significant differences between Ontario and Michigan cities are noted where appropriate.

THE ROLE OF ECONOMIC DEVELOPMENT PROFESSIONALS

It seems clear that economic development decisions are largely the prerogative of economic development professionals. Of the economic development directors surveyed, 47% believe that they are most influential in initiating economic development activities. Another 9% state that the economic development commissioner is most influential. Only 4% say that mayors are most influential, while 11% point to the city manager as being most involved in initiating economic development efforts. The influence of economic development professionals appears greater in Canada; however, the modal response in both cases is "economic development directors" and the difference in response rates is not statistically significant (see Table 6-1).

City administrators/managers and mayors tend to agree that the locus of policy initiation lies with economic development professionals, although at slightly lower levels. Mayors in both nations were evenly divided between saying that economic development directors and themselves were most influential (33% for Ontario and 36% for Michigan). A personal interview with one mayor suggested a likely balance in roles. In this case the mayor saw his role as being one of "public relations" which would include not only selling projects to the community at large, but also to prospective firms and higher levels of government. Thus, the economic development director would do the "technical stuff" and the mayor would act as a promoter.

While the largest percentage of city managers in Ontario indicated that economic development directors were most influential, the modal response among Michigan managers was that they were most influential in policy initiation. The next highest percentages suggested that a mix of officials or business leaders were most influential. Only a handful of city managers in Michigan identified the economic development director as being most influential. Thus, there appears to be fairly widespread agreement that the locus of power in initiating local economic development policy lies with the economic development directors, with the exception being the perception of city managers in Michigan. However, it is worth noting that in most Michigan cities responding, there was no separate economic development director and the manager had significant responsibility for development efforts.

Further, citizens appear to play little role in developing economic development policies. A third or less of economic development directors, managers/administrators, and mayors agreed or strongly agreed that citizens were fairly active in developing economic strategies. Reaction to city council's involvement in policy-making is mixed, with fairly even percentages indicating that they do and do not play a significant part. Overall, chief executives suggest a smaller role for council in economic development than do the economic development professionals--however, the modal response in each case suggests a more limited role. It is important to note, however, that the role of advisory boards which would include citizens appeared quite important in reducing political uncertainty and stress. In interviews, development professionals suggested that such boards "can be your best buffer" between the professional and the political process in that they can be used as trouble shooters and provide support for projects.

Economic development directors also strongly believe that projects are primarily guided by the professional training of decision-makers, and that such decisions are mostly left to economic development administrators. They also indicate that professional staff is more important in initiating economic development policies than are elected officials. In face-to-face interviews, economic development professionals in both nations indicated that the initiation for projects came primarily from the economic development organization, be it a city department or public-private commission. Obviously, approval for most projects ultimately comes from the city council; however, the professionals frame the debate, provide and structure the pertinent information, and establish the cooperation of the various other department heads necessary to the project. Further, they tended to see their role as that of broker or facilitator. The description of the process for establishing an industrial park in one city is illustrative of the balance between appointed and elected officials for fairly routine matters. First, the economic development commission selects an appropriate site. The commissioner would then discuss with and gain the cooperation of the other city departments likely to be involved in project implementation: public works, utilities, planning, zoning, property division, and city attorney/solicitor. The city administrator/manager would sign-off and then the fully developed proposal would go before city council. And, the council "always approves" what the Commission wants.[2]

The responses of managers/administrators and mayors are similar in most cases, with officials in Ontario exhibiting somewhat higher agreement that decisions are driven by professionals. Only in the case of mayors in Michigan did the majority suggest that economic development decisions were not primarily left to professional bureaucrats. This suggests a basic consensus on these points even among officials with different roles. Finally, it should be noted that the response rates for chief executives are extremely low--their perceptions are included here only to provide a bit of a reality check on the economic development officials, particularly as it relates to their own influence in the decision-making process.

ENVIRONMENTAL TURBULENCE

Economic development directors have somewhat mixed perceptions of the extent of environmental turbulence (see Table 6-2). Of those surveyed, most feel optimistic about the future of the national economy; however, only a few feel that they can affect the local economy through their actions. In other words, "we do the best we can" in the face of environmental uncertainty and political pressure, said one official. Or, in a bit more colorful language, "our affect is so small--we're just out there doing what you would do in the wind." And, a majority feel that there is focus in their city's economic development efforts. Still, economic development directors do appear to evidence a fairly strong street-level orientation; they do not believe that citizens and other officials understand what they do and indicate that businesses play one city off against others, adding to environmental stress.

The lack of understanding among other officials such as the mayor and city council can actually be a dual-edged sword. As one community development professional stated during a focus group session, "I'm the only one in the city who knows my job--if I mess something up there is no one to help me. The upside, however, is that there is no one to catch it either." Thus, while lack of understanding on the part of citizens and elected officials can create stress due to unclear goals among other things, it can also insulate professional decision-making to a certain extent. Economic development professionals are optimistic about national trends and feel focused in their local development efforts, but their attitudes reflect perceptions of turbulence in the environment.

RELIANCE ON DECISION RULES

Reactions to the simple question "how do you deal with turbulence and stress" elicited almost a "gallows humor" among community development officials at a focus group session. Responses ranged from "ask my wife" and "it's awful" to "many in our field are long dead--we're just the survivors." Survey data suggest that the reliance on decision rules to lessen environmental stress is also evident, with "shooting at everything" somewhat more prevalent than goal displacement. Many economic development directors reported feeling pressured to use all types of techniques available and permitted by law, and described strong demand for incentives by business. But, only a third granted all requests for incentives. The mean percentage of cities "shooting at everything that flies" is 52%.

Of the respondents, an average of 43% indicate goal displacement behavior, with a majority taking on projects that pleased others in the city but that may not meet long-term goals. Over a third focused on "busywork" rather than goal directed efforts or major projects. And, a quarter relied on showcase projects to foster the impression that things are being done. Further, many feel that they must go from emergency to emergency rather than focusing on long term goals, and over half feel pressured to show immediate results. In

90

discussions with development officials, goal displacement behavior was clearly expressed. For example, "because of politics we end up doing things which don't necessarily meet real goals," stated one professional. Similarly, another suggested that "60% of what I do is politically CYA. It has nothing to do with planning, or what's right --it's about politics, whose projects get funded." It also appears that a good bit of time is spent "documenting what you advised the elected officials to do" to spread the risk and hence, blame, if a project or policy goes wrong. As another official stated, "I've seen a lot of economic developers crash and burn on the need to take credit for projects instead of pushing the stakeholders out front."

While Ontario and Michigan cities show no difference in their tendency toward goal displacement, Michigan cities are significantly more likely to grant any request for incentives by firms. The difference may well reflect the greater discretion granted cities in Michigan to employ financial incentives.

RATIONAL DECISION-MAKING

Overall, a slight majority of cities have an economic development plan and almost one half of economic development directors believe that the plan shapes decision-making. Given this, however, little evaluation occurs to determine if policies are actually meeting stated goals. Further, few respondents could describe their method of forecasting or assessment as being systematic, such as cost/benefit analysis or forecasting. On average, then, 35% of the economic development directors are engaging in rational planning and evaluating behaviors.

Ontario cities are significantly more likely to have an economic development plan. As noted previously, however, the existence of such plans in Ontario is more a product of provincial requirements than an actual commitment to rational planning. The tendency to evaluate is low in both cases. In short, decision rules such as shooting and goal displacement, with average usage rates of 52% and 43%, clearly outweigh planning and evaluation (35%) in local economic decision-making.

SUMMARY

This analysis highlights the importance of the environment of decision-makers and indicates how perceptions of the environment can affect subsequent decision-making processes. Environmental uncertainty creates stress for economic development decision-makers and results in the use of coping techniques such as shooting and goal displacement behavior. The reliance on decision rules outweighs rational planning and evaluation by a considerable margin. The next chapter builds on this analysis to create a more complete model of economic development policy-making than has been suggested in the literature to date.

TABLE 6-1

Actor most influential in initiating economic development activities:

	Respondent					
Actor	ED Director		Manager		Mayor	
	ONT	MI	ONT	MI	ONT	MI
ED Director	71	28	46	07	33	36
ED Commissioner	07	09	00	10	11	00
Manager	05	15	09	35	00	09
Mayor	10	17	18	07	33	36
Business leader	02	13	09	14	11	09
Other	05	17	18	21	11	00
	N=95		N=40		N=20	

Citizens are fairly active in having input in developing economic initiatives:

	Respondent					
	ED Director		Manager		Mayor	
	ONT	MI	ONT	MI	ONT	MI
Strongly agree	00	00	09	00	00	00
Agree	15	33	18	35	22	27
Undecided	24	22	27	21	00	36
Disagree	46	44	36	41	44	27
Strongly disagree	15	00	09	03	33	09

City council takes an active role in evaluating economic development initiatives:

	Respondent					
	ED Director		Manager		Mayor	
	ONT	MI	ONT	MI	ONT	MI
Strongly agree	00	07	18	07	00	36
Agree	37	44	55	45	33	27
Undecided	12	17	00	28	11	09
Disagree	46	30	27	21	44	27
Strongly disagree	05	02	00	00	11	00

Table 6-1 (continued)
Economic development decisions are
mostly left to professional administrators:

	ED Director		Respondent Manager		Mayor	
	ONT	MI	ONT	MI	ONT	MI
Strongly agree	02	07	09	00	22	18
Agree	59	50	73	41	33	18
Undecided	10	17	00	24	00	18
Disagree	27	26	18	31	44	36
Strongly disagree	02	00	00	03	00	09

Economic development projects are
guided by the professional training of
decision makers:

	ED Director		Respondent Manager		Mayor	
	ONT	MI	ONT	MI	ONT	MI
Strongly agree	02	04	00	03	11	09
Agree	51	35	36	31	56	46
Undecided	32	28	27	45	11	36
Disagree	12	32	36	21	22	09
Strongly disagree	02	02	00	00	00	00

Professional staff is more important in initiating
economic development policies than elected
officials:

	ED Director		Respondent Manager		Mayor	
	ONT	MI	ONT	MI	ONT	MI
Strongly agree	32	04	09	07	22	18
Agree	44	43	55	31	11	27
Undecided	12	35	18	35	56	09
Disagree	12	17	18	17	11	27
Strongly disagree	00	02	00	10	00	18

TABLE 6-2

Decision Rules	SA	A	U	D	SD
The city pursues all types of incentives allowed by law.	16	52	12	19	02
The city usually grants any incentives requested by firms.	07	27	14	30	23
There is a strong demand by businesses for economic development incentives.	15	40	20	23	01
I have to undertake activities just to please citizens/officials even if they accomplish little.	04	52	20	22	02
Much of what I do is busy work that has little to do with really generating development.	01	34	26	33	06
Cities emphasize showcase projects to distract from a lack of progress on more fundamental problems.	00	25	32	39	04
I spend too much time firefighting rather than on longer-term problems.	04	43	26	24	02

Rational Decision-Making

Economic Development Plan	Ontario 68% Michigan 38%
Structured system for evaluation	Ontario 37% Michigan 13%
Structured system for selecting among policy alternatives	Ontario 25% Michigan 16%

	SA	A	U	D	SD
The economic development plan guides decisions regarding policies and projects.	04	40	27	22	06

1. A previous and much more limited version of this argument was published as Decision Rules in Local Economic Development, *Urban Affairs Quarterly*, 28 (March 1993): 501-513.

2. This process and the certainty of council approval were described by both the mayor and economic development commissioner within the same city.

REFERENCES

Allison, G.T. 1971. *Essence of decision: Explaining the Cuban missile crisis.* Boston: Little, Brown and Company.

Beaumont, E.F. and Hovey, H. 1985. State, local and federal economic development practices: New federal patterns, chaos or what? *Public Administration Review* 45: 327-332.

Bingham, R.D. 1976. *The adoption of innovation by local government.* Lexington, MA: D.C. Heath & Co.

Bollens, S.A. 1990. Constituencies for limitation and regionalism. *Urban Affairs Quarterly* 26 (September): 46-67.

Bowman, A.O'M. 1988. Competition for economic development among southeastern cities. *Urban Affairs Quarterly* 4 (June): 511-527.

Brierly, A. 1986. State economic development policy choices. Paper presented at the Annual Meeting of the Midwest Political Science Association, Chicago, IL.

Churchman, C.W. 1969. *The systems approach.* New York: Delacorte Press.

Doig, J.W. 1987. Coalition-building by a regional agency: Austin Tobin and the Port of New York Authority. In C.N. Stone and H.T. Sanders (eds.), *The politics of urban development* (73-104). Lawrence: University Press of Kansas.

Feiock, R.C. 1989. The adoption of economic development policies by state and local governments: A review. *Economic Development Quarterly* 3 (August): 266-270.

Fernandez, J. and Pincus, J. 1982. *Troubled suburbs: An exploratory study.* Santa Monica, CA.: Rand Corporation.

Green, G.P. and Fleischmann, A. 1991. Promoting economic development: A comparison of central cities, suburbs and nonmetropolitan communities. *Urban Affairs Quarterly* 27 (September): 145-154.

Green, R.E. and Brintnall, M.A. 1986. State enterprise zone programs: Variations in structure and coverage. Paper presented at the annual meetings of the Midwest Political Science Association, Chicago, IL and the American Society for Public Administration, Anaheim, CA.

Goldstein, M.L. 1985. Choosing the right site. *Industry Week* 15 (April): 57-60.
Jones, B.D. and Bachelor, L.W. 1984 Local policy discretion and the corporate surplus. In R.D. Bingham and J.P. Blair (eds.), Urban Economic Development 27, *Urban Affairs Annual Reviews.* Beverly Hills: Sage Publications: 245-268.

Jones, B.D. and Bachelor, L.W. (1986/1993). *The sustaining hand.* Lawrence, Kansas: University Press of Kansas.

Jones, B.D., Greenberg, S. and Drew, J. 1980. *Service delivery in the city: Citizen demand and bureaucratic rules.* New York: Longman.

Kantor, P. 1987. The dependent city the changing political economy of urban economic development in the United States. *Urban Affairs Quarterly* 22: 493-520.

96

Karnig, A.K. 1975. Private-regarding policy, civil rights groups, and the mediating impact of municipal reforms. *American Journal of Political Science* 19 (February): 91-106.

Katznelson, I. 1976. The crisis of the capitalistic city: Urban politics and social control. In W.D. Hawley (ed.), *Theoretical perspectives on urban politics* (214-229). Englewood Cliffs: Prentice-Hall, Inc.

Kieschnick, M. 1981. *Taxes and growth: Business incentives and economic development.* Washington: Council of State Planning Agencies.

Levenbach, F.D. 1986. The impact of bureaucratic routines on the political management of the EDA's public works program. Paper presented at the annual meeting of the Midwestern Political Science Association, Chicago, IL.

Levy, J.M. 1981. *Economic development programs for cities, counties, and towns.* New York: Prager.

Lineberry, R.L. and Fowler, E.P. 1967. Reformism and public policies in American cities. *American Political Science Review* 61 (September): 701-716.

Lipsky, M. 1980. *Street level bureaucracy.* New York: Russell Sage Foundation.

Logan, V.R. and Molotch, H.L. 1987. *Urban fortunes: The political economy of place.* Berkeley: University of California Press.

Longoria, T. 1994. Empirical analysis of city limits typology. *Urban Affairs Quarterly* 30 (September): 102-113.

McGowan R.P. and Stevens, J.M. 1983. Local government initiatives in a climate of uncertainty. *Public Administration Review* 43: 127-136.

Meyer, P. 1993. A tale of three (British) cities: economic development politics in Cardiff, Leeds and Glasgow. In D. Fasenfest (ed.), *Community economic development* (122-138). New York: St. Martin's Press.

Molotch, H. and Logan, J.R. 1985. Urban dependencies new forms of use and exchange in U.S. cities. *Urban Affairs Quarterly* 21: 143-170.

Northrop, A. and Dutton, N. 1978. Municipal reform and group influence. *American Journal of Political Science* 22 (August): 691-711.

Pagano, M.A. and Bowman, A.O'M. 1989. Risk assumption and aversion: City government investment in development. Paper presented at the annual meeting of the American Political Science Association, Atlanta, GA.

Pagano, M.A. and Bowman, A.O'M. 1995. *Cityscapes and capital.* Baltimore: Johns Hopkins University Press.

Pelissero, J.P. 1986. Intrametropolitan economic development policies: An exploratory look at suburban competition and cooperation. Paper presented at the annual meeting of the Midwest Political Science Association, Chicago, IL.

Pelissero, J.P. and Fasenfest, D. 1989. Suburban economic development policy. *Economic Development Quarterly* 3 (November): 301-311.

Peterson, P.E. 1981. *City limits*. Chicago: University of Chicago Press.

Reese, L.A. 1991. Municipal fiscal health and tax abatement policy. *Economic Development Quarterly* 5 (February): 23-32.

Reese, L.A. 1992. Explaining the extent of local economic development activity: Evidence from Canadian cities. *Government and Policy* 10: 105-120.

Reese, L.A. 1993. Categories of local economic development techniques: An empirical analysis. *Policy Studies Journal* 21 (Autumn): 492-506.

Reese, L.A. 1993. Decision rules in local economic development. *Urban Affairs Quarterly* 28 (March): 501-513.

Rosenfeld, R.A., Reese, L.A., Georgeau, V., and Wamsley, S. 1995. Community development block grant spending revisited: Patterns of benefit and program institutionalization. *Publius: The Journal of Federalism* 25 (Fall): 55-72.

Rubin, B.M. and Zorn, C.K. 1985. Sensible state and local economic development. *Public Administration Review* 45 (March/April): 333-340.

Rubin, H.J. 1988. Shoot anything that flies; claim anything that falls; conversations with economic development practitioners. *Economic Development Quarterly* 3 (August): 236-251.

Rubin, H.J. 1990. Working in a turbulent environment: Perspectives of economic development practitioners. *Economic Development Quarterly* 4 (May): 113-127.

Rubin, H.J. and Rubin, I. 1987. Economic development incentives: The poor (cities) pay more. *Urban Affairs Quarterly* 23 (December): 37-62.

Schmenner, R.W. 1982. *Making business location decisions*. Englewood Cliffs, NJ: Prentice Hall, Inc.

Schneider, M. 1986. The market for local economic development: The growth of suburban retail trade, 1972-1982. *Urban Affairs Quarterly* 1 (September): 24-41.

Schneider, M. 1989. *The competitive city*. Pittsburgh: University of Pittsburgh Press.

Sharkansky, I. 1970. *The routines of politics*. New York: Van Nostrand Reinhold.

Stone, C.N. 1987. The study of the politics of urban development. In C.N. Stone and H.T. Sanders (eds.), *The politics of urban development* (3-22). Lawrence: University Press of Kansas.

Vogel, R.K. and Swanson, B.E. 1989. The growth machine versus the antigrowth coalition: The battle for our communities. *Urban Affairs Quarterly* 25 (September): 63-85.

Wildavsky, A. 1979. *Speaking truth to power*. Boston: Little, Brown and Company.

Wolman, H. 1988. Local economic development policy: What explains the divergence between policy analysis and political behavior? *Journal of Urban Affairs* 10: 19-28.

CHAPTER 7

A MODEL OF ECONOMIC DEVELOPMENT POLICY-MAKING

This chapter presents an explanatory model of economic development decision-making which reflects the realities of the environment of development professionals and includes the use of decision rules. The model also includes several variables found to be important in prior analyses of local economic development policy outcomes. The analysis proceeds in two stages. The first stage, presented here, posits a model explaining the three decision rule behaviors established earlier; "shooting at everything," goal displacement, and rational planning/evaluation. Chapter 8 then extends the model to predict the actual policies or strategies employed.

THE PROPOSED MODEL
Figure 7-1 portrays a basic model of decision-making based on the economic development literature. The ultimate dependent or outcome variables are the opposing behaviors of rational planning and shooting. Goal displacement is what occurs as decision-makers retreat from rational planning and evaluation toward shooting. The specific relationship between goal displacement and shooting and planning behaviors is portrayed in Figure 7-2.[1] The argument here is that there is a continuum of professional behavior ranging from formal planning to "shooting at anything that flies." Shooting behavior is seen as a conscious response to stress or uncertainty in the environment--competition with other cities, turbulence in goals and expectations, and political pressures such as job security and indirect electoral incentives. As turbulence increases, goal displacement presumably occurs as decision-makers shift toward shooting responses. To summarize very simply:

- if goals are unclear and conflicting;
- if other actors, elected officials, or citizens, do not understand the role of the economic development professional;
- if such officials have differing visions of that role;
- if resources are low and expectations are high; and

- if immediate results are necessary to meet political demands and hence increase job security;
- then, bureaucrats are likely to favor the achievable over the optimal.

To revisit the words of the economic development official, "don't ask me whether tax base has increased or jobs have been created, ask me how many firms I've visited this week." Under conditions of uncertainty, goals shift from what should be done under ideal circumstances to what can be done under real circumstances. To combine the axes, then, as the environment shifts from order (fiscal health, low competition, little political pressure) to chaos (fiscal stress, intercity competition, political pressure), goal displacement shifts behavior along a continuum from planning to shooting.

The line of expected behavior is drawn to indicate the proposition that at any point, the system tends toward displacement. In other words, given any level of stress or chaos in the environment, decision-makers are expected to overreact with more goal displacement behavior, or shooting, in an attempt to stave off further anticipated economic stress and job loss. Further, as formal order decays, the shifts from planning will not be orderly. Increasing disorder is likely to result in panic and overcompensation geared to perceptions of increasing chaos in the future. Uncertainty will lead to even more strenuous attempts to gain some measure of control over the environment.

As in many facets of life, if certain elements are beyond control, additional effort is made to achieve greater control over those elements still within the sphere of influence. For an economic development professional, as competition, unemployment, business relocation, and political pressure increase, there will be an even greater tendency to point to accomplishments, however modest or instrumental. Thus, it is expected that goal displacement leads to lower levels of rational planning and greater tendencies to shoot at anything and everything, and, concomitantly, taking credit for anything that happens.

Moving backwards in the model hypothesized in Figure 7-1, the literature suggests that environmental turbulence should increase goal displacement in the manner described above (Lipsky, 1980; Rubin, 1990). Further, to the extent professionals are involved in decision-making, turbulence and displacement should be reduced. The rationale here is that greater reliance on professionals should insulate the decision-making process from political/electoral pressures somewhat, at least in a direct sense. In the same way that certain taxing and budgetary decisions are often handled "off-cycle" within professional circles and away from a critical and likely hostile public eye, keeping economic development decisions within a "cozy triangle" should reduce stress and increase the predictability of the entire enterprise. Indeed, the whole notion of cozy or iron policy triangles or subsystems suggests that decision-making within a small group--of professionals or bureaucrats, politicos, and affected interests--will serve to shelter the issue from public controversy.

Environmental turbulence is a function of a variety of factors. Stress factors such as intercity competition and poor fiscal health should increase turbulence (Bingham, 1976; Bowman, 1988; Rubin, 1990). Governmental structure should also contribute to environmental stress since it determines the organizational framework for the decision-making process. Unreformed political systems should increase turbulence, given the greater politicization of the environment and the increased pressure from and access to localized groups (Lineberry and Fowler, 1967; Karnig, 1975; Heilig and Mundt, 1984; Meier and England, 1984; Svara, 1990; Reese, 1991; Polinard et al., 1994).

Finally, the extent of resources devoted to and the level of professionalism in economic development should affect turbulence. Specifically, more resources devoted to economic development and increased professionalism should reduce turbulence (Pelissero and Fasenfest, 1989; Reese, 1991). In turn, higher levels of economic/fiscal health should increase the amount of resources available for economic development. Competition with neighboring communities should also increase the resources devoted to economic development, as cities strive to stay in the game. Finally, more politicized or less reformed cities are also expected to devote higher levels of resources to economic development because of their greater responsiveness to citizen and business pressures. The relationships among the variables are displayed in Figure 7-1. The following sections explain how each of the variables are measured or operationalized.

MEASUREMENT ISSUES

Ten of the 11 variables in the model are measured by using indexes; only the presence of a mayor is represented by a single measure. The original survey was created with the goal of measuring concepts like shooting behavior, goal displacement, and planning. Factor analysis was performed on individual survey questions--representing shooting, rationality, goal displacement, turbulence, the extent of bureaucratic influence on decisions, resources, professionalism, competition, reformism, and fiscal health--to ascertain empirically that the questions were measuring concepts in the anticipated manner.

Table 7-1 presents complete findings from the factor analysis. Factor analysis was employed since it identifies groups of variables which are related to some exogenous concept not included in the analysis--in this case the conceptual behaviors of shooting, goal displacement, and so on. The cutpoint for loading on a factor was .50 in all cases. The standard SPSS software default modes of listwise deletion of missing values, principal component analysis, and varimax rotation were employed. There was only one case where a variable loaded on more than one factor and it was included in the factor on which the loading was the strongest.[2]

The *Fiscal Health Index* is composed of the extent of perceived growth in the economy over the past five years, city population, employment rates, and median family income levels.[3] Thus, cities with greater perceived growth, larger populations, low unemployment, and higher median incomes rate higher on the index of fiscal health. This represents communities where individual prosperity is higher and where officials perceive growth to have occurred. While the population and income data come from census records, the measure of perceived growth is really most critical here, quite apart from objective figures. The focus here is on the role of professionals and how they react to their environment. Thus, their perceptions of growth are as important as actual growth. The fact that the perceptual and objective data load on the same factor suggests that in most cases decision-makers are realistic in assessing their fiscal environment.

Property values and tax rates were also examined as possible measures of fiscal health but loaded on a separate factor representing cities with higher values and higher rates. This index did not correlate with any variables further along in the model and was not included in any subsequent analysis.

Competition between cities is measured by two questions relating to perceived competition within the state or province and with cities outside of the state/province. Cities higher on the *Competition Index* are perceived to be in greater competition with other cities, both internally and across the border.

The analysis of governmental structure involved two variables. At-large elections and nonpartisan elections loaded on one factor, creating a *Reformed Government Index*.[4] The presence of a mayor did not load here and was analyzed as a separate variable.

The *Turbulence Index* measures stress in the environment; the survey questions were based on those employed by Rubin (1988) to measure the same concept. The index reflects agreement or disagreement with the following statements: there is little one can do to better the local economy since economic problems are national in scope, businesses and industries often play one locality off against another, there is little focus and direction in our economic development efforts, and citizens have no idea of what an economic development practitioner should do. Agreement with these questions indicates perceived turbulence in the environment, reflecting feelings of helplessness, lack of direction and understanding, and stress produced by competition.

The *Resources Index* is comprised of the number of individuals working solely or principally (at least 70% of the time) on economic development activities, and the percentage of time the director of economic development works on economic development activities. This second measure is particularly important since economic development directors often have other duties beyond economic development per se, such as community development, housing, and planning.[5]

The extent of professionalism in economic development is measured by a *Professionalism Index* comprised of whether the economic development director or commissioner has an undergraduate or graduate degree, whether they belong to professional planning or economic development associations, and the extent to which the economic development professional is seen as most influential in initiating economic development policies. Education and affiliation have been found to significantly affect how officials frame economic development issues (Meyer, 1993).

The extent to which economic development decisions are left to professionals was measured by a *Bureaucratic Index* representing agreement with the following statements; economic development projects are guided by the professional training of decision-makers, economic development decisions are mostly left to professional administrators such as an economic development director or commissioner, and professional staff is more important in initiating economic development policies than elected officials. This index measures locus of control; cities high on the index are more likely to leave economic development decision to the "professionals."

The *Goal Displacement Index* is comprised of agreement or disagreement with the following statements: I have to spend too much of my time "firefighting" rather than on longer term economic development projects, people in this community too often judge my work on immediate results rather than long-run accomplishments, much of what I do is "busywork" that has little to do with really generating economic development, I have to undertake some activities just to please constituents or other officials even if I think these activities accomplish little, and the city emphasizes showcase projects to distract from a lack of progress in solving more fundamental economic development problems. Agreement with these statements indicates the subversion of long term goals by immediate pressures and demands, thus producing goal displacement.

The *Rational Planning and Evaluation Index* is comprised of four variables: whether the city has an economic development plan, whether officials indicate that the plan guides actual economic development activity, if the city uses systematic procedures prior to policy implementation to aid in policy choice, and whether the city evaluates policies once they are in place to see if they are meeting goals. Higher scores on this index portray a city where planning is not a rhetorical activity, they have a plan and it drives decisions, and evaluation is employed to assess the attainment of planned goals.

Finally, the *Shooting Index* reflects the extent of agreement with the following statements; the city pursues all types of economic development incentives allowed by the state/province, there is strong demand by business for economic development incentives from this city, and the city usually grants any incentives requested by prospective firms. Cities responding affirmatively represent a situation where firms need only ask for incentives and they are granted, and where all possible incentives are offered. Demand is important here since research has indicated that many cities agree to all requests for economic development incentives (Reese, 1991). Therefore, greater demand leads to more incentives. Since the process is driven by the desires of firms, it represents a shooting dynamic which is inherently reactive in nature.

ONTARIO/MICHIGAN DIFFERENCES

There are some differences between cities in Ontario and Michigan, as suggested in Chapter 6. Cities in Ontario are significantly higher on the fiscal health index, although they are also significantly more likely to be perceived in competition with cities both in the province and in the states. While

Ontario cities are more likely to be reformed, with nonpartisan and at-large elections, they are also significantly more likely to have a mayor as opposed to a city administrator or manager. Canadian cities devote greater resources to economic development and are more likely to leave decisions to professionals. Officials in the two nations are equally likely to perceive environmental turbulence, have professional backgrounds, and engage in goal displacement. Regarding decision-making processes, cities in Ontario are significantly more likely to engage in rational planning and are thus less likely to "shoot at anything that flies."

ANALYSIS

Path analysis was employed to examine the model portrayed in Figure 7-1, using the indexes described above. As such, it "begins with a set of structural equations which represent the structure of interrelated hypotheses in a theory" and follows standard statistical procedures for tracing paths (Bohrnstedt, 1982, p. 441). Such analysis is based on the assumption that error correlations for endogenous variables are zero, thus allowing the use of ordinary least squares regression to estimate the path coefficients (beta weights). It is also assumed that random disturbances are not correlated with each other and/or with exogenous variables.

Initial analysis of the model resulted in fairly unsatisfactory results; extremely low r^2 values and beta coefficients. The overall explanatory power of the model as depicted was very weak and few variables acted as significant predictors of decision-making processes (see Appendix A for path data on the original model).

As an alternative, Figure 7-3 portrays the "best-fitting" model for the data at hand. Criteria for establishing the most robust model were the following; r^2 for the individual paths, parsimony in explanatory variables, and variables with the strongest betas. The best-fitting model meets these criteria and provides the most robust explanation of the three decision-making behaviors; goal displacement, rationality, and shooting. While the best-fitting model presented in Figure 7-3 and described below is similar to the initial model, it appears that the relationships between explanatory variables are more complex than anticipated by a review of the literature. Table 7-2 provides complete data for the path analysis in Figure 7-3.

The Impact of Fiscal Health and Governmental Structure

It is clear from the model that structure and fiscal health are both important in determining decision-making procedures. This supports earlier work suggesting that economics alone as an explanation for policy outcomes is far too limiting. What cities do in economic development is not simply a function of economic conditions; governmental structure and decisions about resources can and do play a role.

Governmental structure is likely to have several impacts. Cities with reformed systems devote significantly more resources to economic development and this probably contributes greatly to perceptions of less

104

turbulence. Indeed, interviews with economic development professionals consistently elicited concern and stress related to politicized environments. Relations with mayors and council seemed particularly problematic from the perspective of the economic development professional. "Council members are always calling before an election asking, what are you doing? Why? Once the election is over the pressure subsides--but we still can't really relax." Another suggested that "if the elected officials want the project, they are going to do it" regardless of professional input. And, electoral chances only serve to enhance the stress; "the heck of it is, when you change elected officials then you really have uncertainty." While reformism is not significantly related to more professional economic development agencies, the presence of a mayor as opposed to a city manager or administrator significantly reduces professionalism. This particular relationship was noted by Svara, who found that department heads in mayor cities were less likely to emphasize rational decision-making and more likely to stress service provision for particularized constituencies. Thus, department heads in such systems are "less professional rather than unprofessional in filling their duties" (1990, p. 218). In short, governmental structure impacts many of the basic parameters of decision-making; resources, professionalism, and, ultimately, turbulence.

Fiscal health also shapes the decision-making environment to an extent. Cities with more robust economies are significantly more likely to devote greater resources to economic development. However, beyond this effect, fiscal health and intercity competition are more likely to affect decision-making procedures directly. Decision-makers in cities with high levels of competition are significantly more likely to evidence goal displacement and shooting behavior. In cities with weak economies, significantly more shooting behavior is also likely to occur. In short, it appears that environmental factors such as a weak economy and perceived strong competition directly increase displacement and shooting behaviors. Governmental structure, however, influences the parameters of decision-making which has impacts later in the model.

Finally, some of the environmental and structural factors are interrelated. Such relationships have been excluded from the model for the sake of clarity, however. Specifically, officials in reformed cities perceive significantly higher levels of competition. There is no obvious *a priori* reason for this. There could be a third variable such as age or extent of land available for development in a community which accounts for this. However, the relationship has no real impact further in the model. Similarly, cities with mayors are more likely to be fiscally healthy, again likely an artifact of some other variable not present in the model.

The Importance of Resources

The amount of resources devoted to economic development appears quite important in predicting decision-making processes. First, greater resources significantly reduce perceived turbulence. At the same time, the amount of resources is also directly related to the extent of rational planning and evaluation. Indeed, in interviews, economic development officials indicated a telling list of activities they would undertake if they had additional resources: more pro-active planning, more targeting of firms for incentives, analysis of market targets, local market analysis, more focused efforts. The effects of additional resources should not be overstated, however, since officials also indicated that additional resources would allow them to do more of the same things they were already doing. Indeed, that resources directly increase goal displacement is troubling. In short, while greater resources appear to increase planning and evaluation, the affect on goal displacement is less clear. On the one hand, greater resources lessen turbulence which seems to reduce the need of local decision-makers to stress showcase projects or pursue projects with immediate results but long-term uncertainty. Increased resources alone, absent a reduction in environmental turbulence, appears only to allow officials the opportunity to do more busywork and showcase projects along with planning and evaluation. It is useful to note that increased resources does not lead to shooting behavior, however. Thus, while there may be a greater opportunity for busywork--perhaps due to additional staff--this does not translate into embracing all types of economic development techniques indiscriminately. Again, the connection between resources and rational planning may serve to limit the tendency to shoot at everything.

Professionalism and the Role of Bureaucrats
First, it should be noted that the index measuring the extent to which decisions are left to bureaucrats is not included in the model in Figure 7-3. This is the case because it was not related to any other variables in the model except competition (positively). The level of professionalism among decision-makers is important, however. Increased professionalism is likely to reduce goal displacement, which in turn increases rational planning and evaluation.

In interviews, one official indicated that increased training has broadened the economic development profession generally to include more female and minority professionals and that it is gradually changing the idea of what economic development is. In the past, "if it didn't belch smoke, it wasn't economic development." Increased professionalism has led to the consideration of a broader set of goals. And, "under the old style economic development you're always successful because whatever you did was the success you claimed." Greater professionalism has led, along with broader goals, to more evaluation of stated goals. Thus, it is not surprising that the path from professionalization leads through less goal displacement to greater rational planning and evaluation. Somewhat surprisingly, resources devoted to economic development do not seem to impact levels of professionalism. It appears that only cities with managers are associated with increased bureaucratic professionalism and, hence, less goal displacement.

Environmental Turbulence

Perceived turbulence in the environment significantly increases the extent of goal displacement on the part of decision-makers. Feelings of hopelessness, that businesses have the upper hand, and that there is little understanding of the role of economic development officials increase the tendency for busywork and showcase activities. In a sense, by keeping visually active, the professional attempts to deal with ambiguities and uncertainty about his/her role. Discussions with local development officials highlighted the impact of uncertainty, particularly in relation to the interplay between elected and appointed actors. Extreme turbulence may accompany pivotal events or major projects where decision-making tends to be shifted from appointed to elected officials. As one official suggested, "council doesn't care about every program or project--only certain things become political or proceed in a manner which is outside of things which are decent and normal." This shift in locus of control may also serve to reduce goal displacement, particularly in relation to busywork and firefighting, as decisions are moved into the hands of elected officials, often the mayor.

Decision-Making Outcomes

To summarize briefly, the extent of goal displacement is significantly increased by competition between cities and turbulence or stress in the environment. This strongly suggests the operation of a street-level bureaucratic mentality where stress and uncertainty increase the use of decision rules. Indeed, as uncertainty increases, one official noted, "I just don't do risky things." Increasing professionalism appears to mitigate these effects to an extent. That reformed systems also reduce goal displacement through resources and professionalism is interesting. Conversations with economic developers shed some light on the dynamics of these connections beyond what is apparent in the data. Professionalism along with less "politicized" systems seems to reduce turbulence and goal displacement. Greater knowledge on the part of economic development professionals vis-à-vis elected officials can be empowering, place more discretion with the professional, and reduce uncertainty. Thus, "if they [elected officials] don't know about the details of the project they are more intimidated by you." Further, it appears that this dynamic may operate even more fully if outside consultants are hired to work with or provide input into professional activities. "Sometimes you (the economic development professional) are just talking to a rock, sometimes the officials believe outside consultants more. And, the more the city pays the consultants, the more elected officials believe them."

There appears to be a general sense that elected officials serve to gum up the works, and in combination with citizen pressure, can push economic development decision-making outside the comfortable and predictable arena of professional control, again creating greater uncertainty. "Political issues are created all the time as individuals try to break into local government power--someone wanting to be elected to council grabs an issue and blows it up." The bottom line from both interview and survey data appears to be that if you reduce politics you reduce uncertainty and hence goal displacement, again accounting for the relationship between unreformed structures and turbulence noted previously.

The relationship between goal displacement and subsequent behaviors is not precisely as predicted in Figure 7-1. While higher levels of goal displacement lead to significantly less rational planning and evaluation, as expected, there is no significant relationship between displacement and shooting behavior. It appears that while turbulence produces a shift from rational planning, the tendency to shoot is directly affected only by competition and fiscal health. Cities in competition with others and in poor fiscal health are more likely to attempt everything and anything to induce development, regardless of any other factors. This dynamic was clearly evident in the reactions of one local official. Upon hearing that a neighboring community was offering relocation subsidies for employees of in-coming firms, she said, "I didn't know they were doing that, if we had known we would have done it too." In this way, competition leads directly to shooting at everything.

SUMMARY

Several general conclusions about decision-making can be drawn from this analysis.

- Economic determinism falls short as an explanation of economic development decision-making; governmental structural factors such as reformism also play a role.
- The amount of resources devoted to economic development can reduce turbulence, thus reducing goal displacement and increasing rationality.
- Increased levels of professionalism reduce the tendency for goal displacement.
- Fiscal health and intercity competition directly increase shooting behavior; decision-makers in cities stressed in this manner will shoot regardless of other factors.

It appears that cities under extreme stress are going to "shoot at anything" regardless of resources, professionalism, and locus of control. This, in a sense, is the bad news. A very poor economy is determinant in large part and drives decision-makers toward any and all activities which might attract or retain fiscal base and, hopefully, jobs. However, the good news is that cities not in such severe straits can reduce the tendency to shoot at anything by committing increased resources to economic development and fostering a more professional approach to decision-making. This interaction between external environment and internal control was superbly summarized by one local professional who suggested that his role was essentially that of a "midwife"; "that's what we basically are, the gestation period is a long one but we're just trying to help produce something." In this manner the external environment, be it competition or fiscal health, structure the condition of the city. However, local actors, structures, and politics then operate to either facilitate or hamper this essential condition.

These findings, however, do not address the ultimate question; what difference does it make? Do cities using more rational decision-making procedures employ different and/or "better" economic development incentives and policies? Do decision-making procedures have an impact on policy outcome? These issues are addressed in the next chapter.

TABLE 7-1
Factor Analysis

Index	Factor Loading
Fiscal Health Index	
Perceived growth	.66
Population	.61
Employment rates	.81
Median family incomes	.88
Competition Index	
Perceived competition within state/province	.88
Perceived competition across the border	.86
Reformed Government Index	
At-large elections	.90
Nonpartisan elections	.87
Turbulence Index	
There is little one can do to better the local economy since economic problems are national in scope	.63
Businesses and industries play one city off against another	.56
There is little focus or direction in economic development efforts	.71
Citizens have no idea what an economic development professional should do	.69
Resource Index	
Number of staff	.79
Economic development director time	.83
Professionalism Index	
Undergraduate degree	.63
Graduate degree	.68
Professional association membership	.64
Economic development director is most influential	.68

Table 7-1 (continued)

Bureaucratic Index

Projects are guided by the professional training of decision-makers	.75
Decisions are left mostly to professional administrators	.81
Professional staff is more important in policy initiation than are elected officials	.67

Goal Displacement Index

I spend too much time firefighting rather than on longer term projects	.69
People judge my work on immediate results	.78
Much of what I do is busywork	.51
I have to undertake some activities just to please others even if they accomplish little	.63
The city emphasizes showcase projects to distract from lack of progress solving fundamental problems	.47

Rational Planning and Evaluation Index

Existence of an economic development plan	.72
The plan guides decision-making	.75
Systematic analysis for decision-making	.60
Post-hoc evaluation	.73

Shooting Index

City pursues all incentives allowed by law	.76
Strong demand for incentives by business	.76
City grants all demands for incentives	.69

TABLE 7-2
Regression Data

	b	Beta	Significance
Resources r^2=.18			
reformism	.22	.22	.03
health	.35	.35	.00
Turbulence r^2=.10			
resources	-.31	-.31	.00
Professionalism r^2=.13			
mayor	-.73	-.36	.00
Goal Displacement r^2=.45			
turbulence	.64	.64	.00
competition	.20	.20	.05
professionalism	-.26	-.24	.01
resources	.23	.24	.02
Rational Planning r^2=.22			
resources	.40	.39	.00
goal displacement	-.30	-.29	.01
Shooting r^2=.22			
competition	.21	.21	.03
health	-.45	-.45	.00

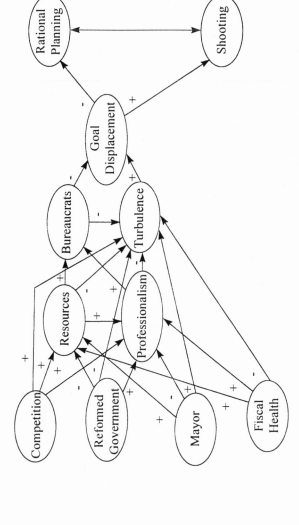

Figure 7.1. Basic Model of Decision-Making

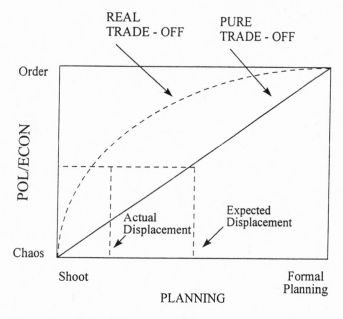

Figure 7.2. The Conceptual Model

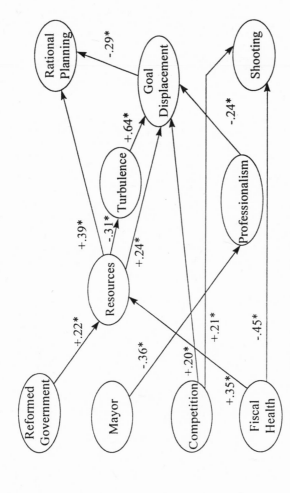

Figure 7.3. Best-Fitting Model of Decision-Making

1. This heuristic was developed with David Fasenfest to explain economic development decision-making as part of an on-going research project.

2. The perception that businesses "played" one city off against another loaded on both the turbulence and goal displacement indexes. It loaded more strongly on the turbulence index and hence was included there.

3. Data for population, unemployment, and median family income were drawn from the 1980 census for Michigan cities and the 1986 census for Ontario cities.

4. The creation of a single reformed index including at-large and nonpartisan elections and a city manager--the standard U.S. indicators of "reform"--is complicated in Canada. As noted previously, Canadian cities have not had a tradition of machine politics, and thus parties were not the target of a "good government" movement. Indeed, in many instances in Canada, local political parties acted as "reformers," stressing social goals along with rational government (Quesnel, 1994).

5. Budget figures would be the best direct indicator of resources committed to economic development, but are almost impossible to obtain in a comparative cross-national effort like this. Economic development funding typically comes from a variety of sources; state and federal pass-throughs, special districts and assessments, public/private sources and so on. Staff and effort directed toward economic development was determined to provide the most comparable and clearly interpretable measure of resources.

REFERENCES

Bingham, R.D. 1976. *The adoption of innovation by local government*. Lexington, MA: D.C. Heath and Co.

Bohrnstedt, G. 1982. *Statistics for social data analysis*. Itasca, IL: Peacock Publishers.

Bowman, A.O'M. 1988. Competition for economic development among southeastern cities. *Urban Affairs Quarterly* 4 (June): 511-527.

Heilig, P. and Mundt, R.J. 1984. *Your voice at city hall: The politics and policies of district representation*. Albany: State University of New York Press.

Karnig, A.K. 1975. Private-regarding policy, civil rights groups, and the mediating impact of municipal reforms. *American Journal of Political Science* 19 (February): 91-106.

Lineberry, R.L. and Fowler, E.P. 1967. Reformism and public policies in American cities. *American Political Science Review* 61 (September): 701-716.

Lipsky, M. 1980. *Street level bureaucracy*. New York: Russell Sage Foundation.

Meier, K.J. and England, R.E. 1984. Black representation and educational policy: Are they related? *American Political Science Review* 78: 392-403.

Meyer, P. 1993. A tale of three (British) cities: Economic development politics in Cardiff, Leeds and Glasgow. In D. Fasenfest (ed.), *Community economic development* (122-138). New York: St. Martin's Press.

Pelissero, J.P. and Fasenfest, D. 1989. Suburban economic development policy. *Economic Development Quarterly* 3 (November): 301-311.

Polinard, J.L., Wrinkle, R.D., Longoria, T. and Binder, N.E. 1994. *Electoral structure and urban policy*. New York: M.E. Sharpe.

Quesnel, L. 1994. Party politics in the metropolis: Montreal 1960-1990. In F. Frisken (ed.), *The changing Canadian metropolis: A public policy perspective*, 581-612, Berkeley: Institute of Governmental Studies Press/Toronto: Canadian Urban Institute.

Reese, L.A. 1991. Municipal fiscal health and tax abatement policy. *Economic Development Quarterly* 5 (February): 23-32.

Rubin, H.J. 1988. Shoot anything that flies; claim anything that falls; conversations with economic development practitioners. *Economic Development Quarterly* 3 (August): 236-251.

Rubin, H.J. 1990. Working in a turbulent environment: Perspectives of economic development practitioners. *Economic Development Quarterly* 4 (May): 113-127.

Svara, J.H. 1990. *Official leadership in the city*. Oxford: Oxford University Press.

117

CHAPTER 8

DECISION-MAKING PROCESSES AND POLICY OUTCOMES

This chapter extends the model developed in Chapter 7 to its logical conclusion; the relationship between city characteristics, decision-making processes, and development strategies. It thus addresses the central issue of what difference the extent of rationality and use of decision rules makes in creating different policy mixes in a community.

CATEGORIZING POLICY OUTCOMES

The first issue to be addressed is that of the dependent variable. While over 50 different techniques are potential dependent variables, such an approach renders analysis logistically difficult and lacks any theoretical or conceptual framework.[1] Thus, the first step in model-building is to categorize development techniques in conceptually logical sets.

In the past, scholars have found it useful to create and employ categories of economic development incentives to facilitate and simplify analysis. Indeed, construction of typologies for a variety of policy areas has occupied political scientists for decades (Lowi, 1964; Peterson, 1981; among many others). Such typologies in economic development have been based on the assumption that certain techniques cluster in natural categories like marketing/promotional activities or financial incentives. Little empirical work has been done, however, to test the validity and utility of such categories as they apply to cities. In other words, the question of whether research typologies match the actual packages of incentives offered by cities remains largely unanswered.

Researchers have pointed to the limits of the use of policy typologies since they are not exogenous variables. As Clingermayer and Feiock note: "Policy types (or the adoption of certain policies) should itself be explained and should not be offered as explanations in themselves" (1990, pg. 141). But empirically based categories would improve the quality of academic research in the field and make analyses more useful to practitioners and scholars alike. It has also been argued that research comparing states by the number of economic development practices employed misses distinctions between different types of techniques (Hanson and Berkman, 1991). Thus, efforts to describe the policy process and explain the use of certain techniques would be enriched by a more realistic definition of dependent variables.

Most of the research on local economic development has explicitly or implicitly employed categories of incentives. Such typologies have utilized a variety of organizing principles: the economic development goals pursued (Dubnick and Bardes, 1983; Matulef, 1987; Pelissero and Fasenfest, 1988), the direct or indirect nature of incentives and business functions targeted (Sternberg, 1987), and the "quantity and distribution of costs and benefits" and the extent of governmental role (Clingermayer and Feiock, 1990). Most typologies reflect the similarity of techniques employed according to economic development method; i.e., marketing, tax incentives, training programs, governmental infrastructure development, for example (Ady, 1984; ICMA, 1989; Hanson and Berkman, 1991; Green and Fleischmann, 1991; Reese, 1992). A brief summary is illustrative.

Sternberg (1987) provides one of the most explicit typologies of economic development incentives, identifying nine sets of economic development policy instruments. These include direct and indirect subsidies, information and exhortation, regulation, impacting crucial industries and institutions, expanding market opportunities, shaping market structure, limiting forms of enterprise, and operating public enterprises or expanding public employment opportunities. These are then categorized by the business function they are meant to address (pgs. 154-160). The logic behind the typology rests in political economy, thus the differentiation by business function.

Clingermayer and Feiock (1990) employed a less detailed but more politically sensitive typology of economic development strategies, explaining the adoption of five policies; industrial development bonds (IDB's), Urban Development Action Grants (UDAG's), business assistance centers, national advertising, and tax abatements. The first two were classified together as policies which represented "diffused costs and concentrated benefits," while assistance centers and advertising denoted a category with more diffuse benefits and concentrated costs. Tax abatements alone represented a category where benefits and costs were not as clear.

Matulef (1987), in discussing strategies for local development and neighborhood revitalization, used an objective-based typology employed in a 1985 National Association of Housing and Redevelopment study. Local incentives were classified as either directed toward coordination of projects or support for development initiatives. Coordination included such things as grantsmanship, consensus building and creating media support. Support services were reduced to nine sub-categories; marketing, community organizing, land-based initiatives, and so on. In a similar vein, Pelissero and Fasenfest (1988) created a typology based on economic development goals. Here, policies were classified as aggressive, regulatory, cooperative, retentive or reactive.

What these studies have in common is the use of typologies based on informed reasoning without empirical verification. Recent typologies presented by Hanson and Berkman (1991) and Boeckelman (1991) of state level economic development initiatives go further and include empirical analysis. In the former, four categories of techniques--capital subsidies, enhancements to return on capital investments, operating subsidies, and enhancements to return on operating outlays--were identified theoretically. The categories were then tested using factor analysis and found to be "weakly confirmed." Similarly, Boeckelman examined 12 state economic development incentives chosen to represent Jackson's maintenance/attraction and creation strategies. While useful, such classification schemes often contain activities not typically conducted by local governments. Indeed, only states typically have the resources and authority to implement sales tax exemptions, right-to-work laws, and tax credits for state products.

There has been limited empirical testing of typologies for local level activities. Rubin (1986) employed empirical analysis to identify two types of economic development incentives--those based on internal actions of local governments and those based on external aid. However, the number of economic development incentives was relatively small (18) and the data were drawn from a single state. Fleischmann, et al. (1992) explored a wider array of economic development tools for cities across the U.S. While extremely useful, the resulting typologies did not include many techniques now more widely employed that are entrepreneurial or demand-side in nature.

CREATING AN EMPIRICAL TYPOLOGY

Factor analysis was employed on the list of 57 economic development incentives included on the questionnaire. The survey initially presented respondents with techniques organized into five categories: marketing activities, governance tools and public infrastructure investment, governmental regulations, land and property management activities, and financial tools. These categories were designed to match those used in the 1989 Economic Development Survey conducted by the International City/County Management Association. The only difference was that the ICMA survey joined governmental regulations with governance tools and infrastructure development, employing four categories. The original categorization from the survey is presented in Appendix B.

Since factor analysis is more robust when theoretically driven, each of the five categories was analyzed separately. Previous research has suggested that the same factors result regardless of whether all 57 techniques are entered together in an analysis or whether they are entered by ICMA category (Reese, 1993). Factor analysis was chosen over other "clustering" techniques such as cluster analysis, because variables rather than cases were being grouped, and multidimensional scaling was used due to the binary nature of the data. Further, this procedure has been successfully employed in other analyses examining clusters of economic development techniques (Rubin, 1986; Boeckelman, 1991; Fleischmann, et al., 1992; Reese, 1993).

The factor analysis identified 13 different categories or "factors" of economic development techniques: two marketing factors, five factors representing governance tools and regulations, three land development/management factors, and three financial factors. These are briefly described in the following section and the results of the complete factor analysis are presented in Table 8-1.[2]

Marketing Techniques and Strategies

The two marketing factors represent a distinction between traditional marketing or promotion efforts and activities which are more entrepreneurial or proactive in nature. In the traditional promotional category are such activities as creation and distribution of brochures, participation in trade shows, visits to prospective firms, and attempts to attract foreign investors or create export markets for local goods. The first three of these activities are practiced by most cities in the sample (over 60%), while the latter two, representing demand-side activity as described by Eisinger, are used by fewer cities. However, they are also fairly common economic development techniques among cities today. Indeed, an average of 60% of cities in Ontario and Michigan engage in techniques in the traditional promotional factor.

The entrepreneurial promotional factor includes such activities as creating liaison committees in which governmental officials work regularly with industry representatives to identify needs, plan for the future, and smooth city/business relations; preparing videos promoting city attributes; planning for special events such as fairs, tours, festivals and the like to promote the city; and using a marketing plan to guide efforts to "sell" the city to external business and tourist interests. These represent more proactive, and in some cases more high-tech activities, and are certainly more labor intensive approaches to economic development. Hence, fewer cities tend to engage in them--on average, 45% of the cities surveyed.

Governance Tools and Regulations

This general category represents the use of city services, regulations, and procedures to either make development easier and/or cheaper or the use of regulations to create a more attractive physical environment in which to live and do business. Thus, the five factors in this area revolve around service and infrastructure, streamlined governmental processes, and regulations to improve the appearance and environment of the city.

Two factors represent service improvements and infrastructure development. The service factor includes improvements in streets to regulate traffic flow, increased sanitation service, and expanded recreation services. The infrastructure factor represents creation or improvement of water and sewage systems. On average, 59% and 48% of the cities engage in each of these factors respectively, making them the most commonly employed economic development strategies in this category.

The environmental improvements factor includes activities designed to enhance the appearance of downtown areas primarily, focusing on retail/service businesses and their clients. These include pedestrian amenities such as walkways and benches; aesthetic improvements such as landscaping, litter control regulations, and historic district regulations to control changes in appearance; and the designation of community improvement areas. A second similar factor represents efforts to regulate the appearance of business areas, including historic district designation, sign regulations, and facade control. Together these represent efforts to make the city more attractive and "user friendly." They are practiced by an average of 44% and 34% of the cities, respectively.

Finally, 38% of the cities engage in activities directed at simplifying city processes for business development. This "streamlined regulations" factor includes "one-stop" permit issuance, simplified building inspection procedures, and modified zoning procedures to facilitate development.

Land-Based Activities

The three land-centered factors include two dealing with development and preparation of sites and one centered around the management of developed land. The site acquisition factor includes land acquisition, lot consolidation, removal of undesired structures, and relocation of existing businesses to other sites. These represent the standard land development techniques practiced for economic development and are conducted by an average of 42% of the cities. The second site development factor represents activities which occur subsequent to initial site preparation; sale or donation of land to developers and rehabilitation of existing structures. These are practiced by an average of 32% of the cities.

Finally, an additional land-based factor includes activities involved in the management of developed sites: office/retail property management, industrial property management, and sale lease-back arrangements. Activities in this factor are employed by an average of 11% of the cities.

Financial Incentives

Under the general rubric of financial incentives, three factors emerge. One revolves around loans, including loan guarantees, loan subsidies, and direct loans to businesses. Such techniques are used by an average of 17% of the cities. The second factor, titled traditional supply-side incentives, includes use of downtown development authorities (DDA), tax increment finance authorities (TIFA), tax abatements and deferred tax payments. An average of 31% of cities use such incentives. The third factor represents more entrepreneurial efforts designed to create new business as opposed to the business attraction focus of traditional supply-side approaches. Activities loading on this factor include use of business incubators, training/retraining programs, and enterprise zones; 15% of the cities on average engage in such activities.

Ontario/Michigan Differences

As suggested earlier, there are some significant differences between Michigan and Ontario cities in the use of these 13 factors. These differences are worth noting again at this point. Cities in the two nations are equally likely to employ techniques in the following economic development factors; streamlined regulations, regulation of appearance, and all of the land factors.

Correlation coefficients were not calculated for traditional financial incentives and business creation. Given the provincial restrictions on financial incentives, Ontario cities do not practice most of the techniques in this factor. Thus, Michigan cities are much more likely to employ traditional supply-side incentives. Very few cities employ training programs and enterprise zones as economic development incentives (19% in Ontario and 4% in Michigan), thus prohibiting the calculation of a correlation coefficient for the constituent business creation factor. However, cities in Ontario are significantly more likely to support training programs and business incubators.

Ontario cities are significantly more likely to use both marketing factors-- standard promotional and entrepreneurial promotional techniques. They are also significantly more likely to engage in service and infrastructure improvements as well as environmental improvements. Michigan cities are significantly more likely to use financial factors, including loans and traditional supply-side incentives. These differences appear to be the result of variation in state/provincial enabling legislation as well as differences in economic development goals.

Predicting Policy Outcomes

To examine the impact of decision-making processes and environmental circumstances on economic development policies, a series of path analyses were run. The best-fitting models for each of the 13 economic development factors were identified, based on the criteria outlined in Chapter 7. The base model remains the same with each of the 13 factors added as the final dependent variable. The decision-making model includes two environmental variables, fiscal health and competition; two structural variables, reformism and the presence of a mayor; resources devoted to economic development; environmental turbulence; the professionalism of decision-makers; and three variables identifying different decision-making procedures--goal displacement, rational planning, and shooting.

Several patterns can be identified from the path analyses of the 13 policy factors. First, only seven of the 11 variables in the base model have significant impacts on policy outcomes. Of these, the extent to which resources are devoted to economic development most frequently predicts the economic development policies employed; in five of the 13 cases resources significantly predict policy outcome. The next most important predictor is the extent of rational planning and evaluation employed, included in three of the 13 paths. The fiscal health of cities, extent of perceived turbulence, and shooting behavior are each included in two of the 13 paths.

The second general pattern is that economic development policies as a whole are not well predicted by any of the models. Indeed, none of the explanatory variables are significantly related to two of the policy factors; business creation and infrastructure development, although the measure of resources is correlated with business creation activity at the .06 level. The following section briefly describes the models for each of the 13 factors.

Marketing Activities

Using the available variables, traditional marketing and entrepreneurial promotion are the two most accurately predicted of the 13 factors, with r^2 values of .40 and .39 respectively (see Figures 8-1 and 8-2). Table 8-2 contains complete data for all of the path analyses. In both factors, the greater the resources devoted to economic development, the greater the use of techniques. Structure also appears important, with more reformed cities using traditional promotional activities to a greater extent. The critical difference in whether traditional or entrepreneurial marketing activities are used appears to be the extent of rationality in the decision-making process. In short, more rationality and less shooting leads to greater use of entrepreneurial promotion activities.

Governance Tools and Infrastructure Development

As noted above, no variables were significant predictors of infrastructure improvements. Further, the only variable significantly correlated with increased service provision was fiscal health; cities with better fiscal health are more likely to enhance service provision as an economic development incentive (see Figure 8-3).

The extent of rational planning and evaluation activity significantly affects the use of regulatory strategies. Greater rationality in economic development decision-making leads to both streamlined regulation procedures for building and site development and increased regulation of the appearance of such sites (see Figures 8-4 and 8-5). This suggests that cities can regulate the characteristics of development while still keeping processes and procedures "user friendly," and that rational planning can lead to such a balance.

Finally, environmental improvements appear to be affected only by the extent of turbulence in the environment. Indeed, greater turbulence reduces such improvements regardless of other city characteristics or decision-making procedures (see Figure 8-6).

Land-Based Activities

A number of variables significantly predict strategies involving the acquisition and development of land for economic development. More reformed cities tend to engage in more site development activities. Turbulence in the environment tends to reduce land development activity, due no doubt to the confluence of uncertainty and long-term character of major projects. Finally, cities relying on decision-rules which stress "shooting" tend to engage more heavily in site acquisition and development (see Figure 8-7).

125

Post-site development activities, selling or donating land to developers, and site management activities are significantly affected only by the extent of resources devoted to economic development. Greater resources increases the use of both types of activities (see Figures 8-8 and 8-9).

Financial Incentives

Similar to the case of site management activities, resources also increase the use of traditional supply-side incentives. This is the only variable significantly correlated with this group of financial incentives (see Figure 8-10).

The use of various loan arrangements is not related to decision procedure or resources. Rather, fiscal health and form of government significantly affect the use of loans (see Figure 8-11). Cities experiencing fiscal stress and without a mayor are significantly more likely to use loans as incentives, perhaps because they tend to be viewed as "low cost" avenues to induce economic development. Again, no variables were significantly correlated with the use of business creation techniques.

SUMMARY

Several conclusions can be drawn from this analysis.

- On the whole, economic development policy choices in cities in Ontario and Michigan are not well explained by the models detailed here. Promotional activities are best predicted, with an r^2 of .40 for traditional techniques and .39 for entrepreneurial activities. The explanatory power for the rest of the economic development policy categories ranges from .05 for streamlined procedures and appearance regulations to .32 for post-site development activities.

- The variables which most frequently predict policy choices are the level of resources devoted to economic development and the extent of rationality in the decision process.

- Greater resource allocations increase the use of traditional and entrepreneurial promotional activities, site management and post-site development, and traditional supply-side incentives.

- Greater reliance on rational planning processes leads to increased use of entrepreneurial promotional activities, streamlined procedures, and appearance regulations. Shooting behavior, on the other hand, reduces the use of entrepreneurial promotional activities and increases site acquisition efforts.

- Environmental factors such as turbulence and fiscal health have some direct impacts on policy outcomes. Turbulence reduces reliance on site acquisition and environmental improvements while poor fiscal health reduces the ability to provide additional services. Cities under fiscal stress, however, are more likely to offer loan arrangements.

- Governmental structure significantly impacts three different categories of incentives. Greater levels of reformism, either the presence of a city

126

manager/administrator or at-large, nonpartisan elections, tend to increase the use of site acquisition, traditional promotion and loan strategies.

While it appears that resources are critical to an understanding of economic development policy-making, the fairly low explanatory power of the decision procedures measured suggests that further research is needed to explore how economic development professionals make policy decisions. Clearly, critical variables are missing from the decision-making models. The final chapter suggests several possible variables which might be considered.

TABLE 8-1
Factor Analysis

Index	Factor Loading	Average % Use
Traditional Promotional		60%
Brochures	.54	
Visits to prospects	.64	
Attract foreign investment	.78	
Trade shows	.77	
Develop export markets	.75	
Entrepreneurial Promotional		45%
Liaison committees	.76	
Videos	.56	
Special events	.61	
Development planning	.67	
Service Improvements		59%
Traffic circulation	.80	
Sanitation	.53	
Recreation	.84	
Environmental Appearance Improvements		44%
Pedestrian amenities	.73	
Esthetic improvements	.73	
Historic district creation	.62	
Community improvements areas	.60	
Litter control	.63	
Streamlined Regulations		38%
One-stop permits	.55	
Streamlined building inspection	.50	
Eased zoning procedures	.57	
Business Appearance		34%
Historic district regulations	.77	
Sign control	.71	
Facade control	.64	
Infrastructure Investment		48%
Water	.93	
Sewage	.92	

Table 8-1 (continued)

Site Acquisition   42%

Land acquisition	.71
Lot consolidation	.80
Demolition	.62
Relocation of business	.55

Post-Acquisition Development   32%

Donation of land to developers	.58
Selling land to developers	.80
Rehabilitation of older buildings	.79

Site Management   11%

Retail property management	.85
Industrial property management	.56
Sale-lease back arrangements	.74

Traditional Financial Incentives   31%

DDA	.70
TIFA	.80
Tax abatements	.62
Deferred tax payments	.60

Loan Arrangements   17%

Loan guarantees	.77
Loan subsidies	.77
Direct loans	.71

Entrepreneurial Financial   15%

Incubators	.60
Training programs	.73
Enterprise zones	.57

TABLE 8-2
Regression Data

	b	Beta	Significance
Traditional Promotion r^2=.40			
reformism	.32	.33	.00
resources	.45	.47	.00
Entrepreneurial Promotion r^2=.39			
rationality	.32	.33	.00
resources	.32	.32	.00
shooting	-.34	-.33	.00
Services r^2=.06			
health	.25	.25	.02
Streamlined Regulations r^2=.05			
rationality	.22	.22	.04
Appearance Regulations r^2=.05			
rationality	.22	.22	.04
Environmental Improvements r^2=.05			
turbulence	-.22	-.22	.03
Site Acquisition r^2=.17			
reformism	.19	.22	.06
turbulence	-.25	-.25	.01
shooting	.22	.19	.03
Post-Site Development r^2=.32			
resources	.36	.31	.03
Site Management r^2=.07			
resources	.26	.27	.01
Traditional Supply-Side r^2=.24			
resources	.53	.49	.00
Loans r^2=.16			
mayor	-.40	-.20	.05
health	-.29	-.29	.00

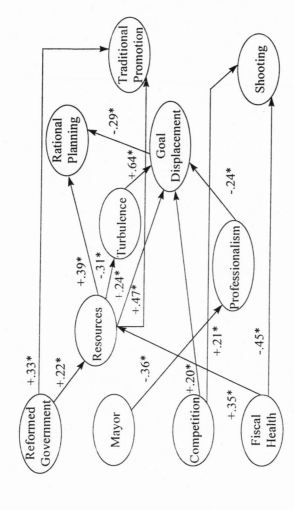

Figure 8.1. Traditional Promotional Activities

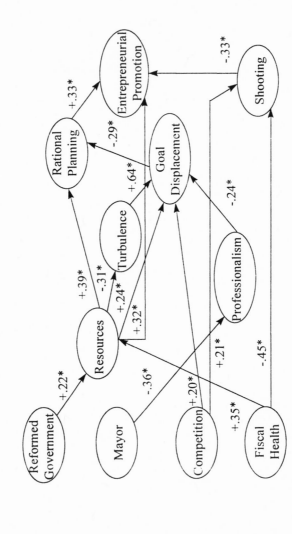

Figure 8.2. Entrepreneurial Promotional Activities

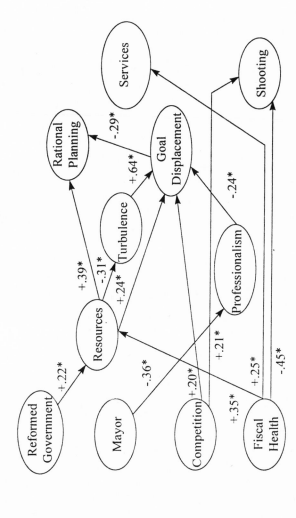

Figure 8.3. Public Service Provision

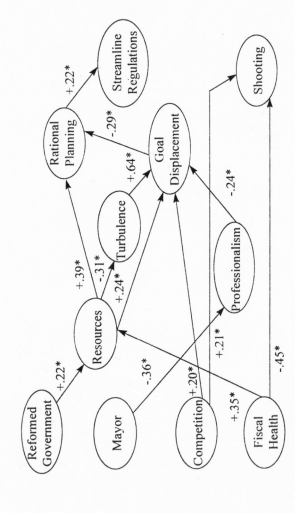

Figure 8.4. Streamline Regulations

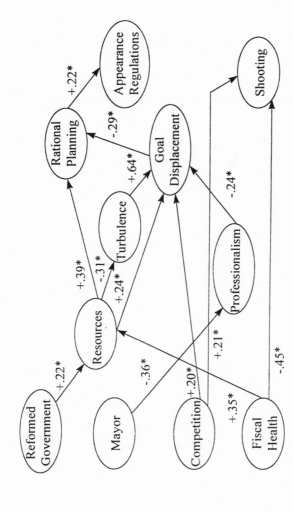

Figure 8.5. Appearance Regulations

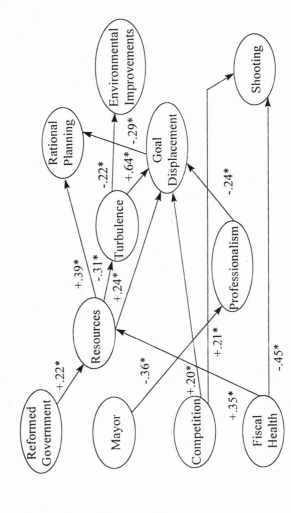

Figure 8.6. Environmental Improvements

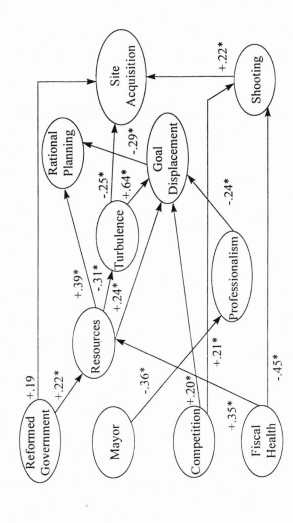

Figure 8.7. Site Acquisition

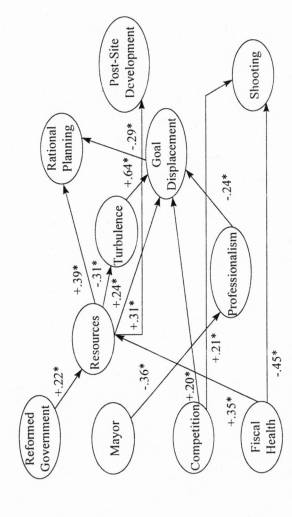

Figure 8.8. Post-Site Development

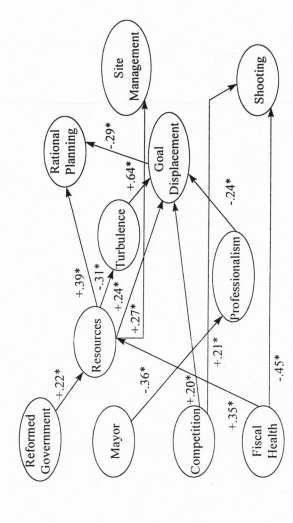

Figure 8.9. Site Management Activities

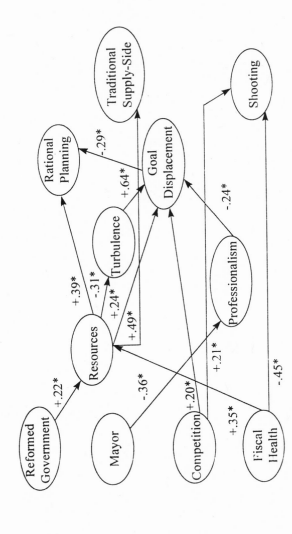

Figure 8.10. Traditional Supply-Side Incentives

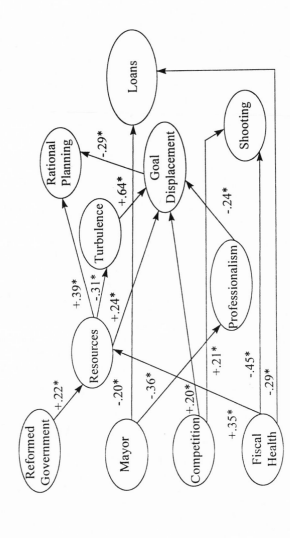

Figure 8.11. Loan Arrangements

1. The total number of techniques on the Ontario survey was 57; 54 were listed on the Michigan version.

2. Only one economic development incentive loaded on more than one factor; land acquisition loaded on both the post-site acquisition and the site acquisition index. It was included only in the latter since the highest factor score occurred there.

REFERENCES

Ady, R.A. 1984. Cited in Joint Economic Committee, U.S. Congress, *Industrial policy movement in the United States; Is it the answer?* Washington, D.C.: Government Printing Office 8 (June): 51-52.

Boeckelman, K. 1991. Political culture and state development policy. *Publius: The Journal of Federalism* 21 (Spring): 49-81.

Clingermayer, J.C. and Feiock, R.C. 1990. The adoption of economic development policies by large cities: A test of economic, interest group, and institutional explanations. *Policy Studies Journal* 18 (Spring): 539-552.

Dubnick, M.J. and Bardes, B.A. 1983. *Thinking about public policy.* New York: John Wiley.

Fleischmann, A., Green, G.P. and Kwong, T.M. 1992. What's a city to do? Explaining the differences in local economic development policies. *The Western Political Quarterly* 45 (September): 677-699.

Green, G.P. and Fleischmann, A. 1991. Promoting economic development: A comparison of central cities, suburbs and nonmetropolitan communities. *Urban Affairs Quarterly* 27 (September): 145-154.

Hanson, R.L. and Berkman, M.B. (1991). A meteorology of state legislative climates. *Economic Development Quarterly* 5 (August): 213-228.

International City Management Association 1989. *Economic Development Survey.* Washington, D.C.: ICMA.

Lowi, T. 1964. American business, public policy, case studies and political theory. *World Politics* (July): 677-715.

Matulef, M.L. 1987. Strategies for economic revitalization. Paper presented at the National Conference of the American Society for Public Administration, Boston, MA.

Pelissero, J.P. and Fasenfest, D. 1989. Suburban economic development policy. *Economic Development Quarterly* 3 (November): 301-311.

Peterson, P.E. 1981. *City limits.* Chicago: The University of Chicago Press.

Reese, L.A. 1992. Local economic development practices in the province of Ontario. *Canadian Public Administration* 35: 237-249.

Reese, L.A. 1993. Categories of local economic development techniques: An empirical analysis. *Policy Studies Journal* 21 (Autumn): 492-506.

Rubin, H.J. 1986. Local economic development organizations and the activities of small cities in encouraging economic growth. *Policy Studies Journal* 14 (March): 363-388.

Sternberg, E. 1987. A practitioner's classification of economic development policy instruments, with some inspiration from political economy. *Economic Development Quarterly* 1 (May): 149-161.

FURTHER EXPLANATION OF LOCAL ECONOMIC DEVELOPMENT POLICY

This book has described, analyzed, and compared local economic development policy in cities in Canada and the United States, and begun the development and testing of a model of local economic development policy-making. The model focused explicitly on the role and environment of economic development professionals and the impact of decision-making practices on local development policy. Five central issues have been addressed:

1) economic development policies and practices in cities in Michigan, USA;
2) economic development policies and practices in cities in Ontario, Canada;
3) the comparability of policies across the border;
4) the role of economic development professionals in local economic development decision-making; and
5) the interaction of economic, political, and professional factors, and their affects on economic development policy.

In short, the book has addressed the following questions:

- What economic development strategies are employed by cities in Ontario and Michigan?
- Are the two sets of cities similar in their approaches to economic development?
- Why do cities pursue certain economic development strategies?
- What is the role of economic development professionals in the decision-making process? and
- What factors explain local economic development policy decisions?

This chapter summarizes the primary findings relating to each of these questions. Further, it highlights key themes presented throughout the book: trends in the use of supply- and demand-side economic development techniques, the role of enabling legislation in the types of policies pursued by communities, the extent of policy convergence between cities in Canada and the U.S., and the role of bureaucrats in local economic development policy-making. Finally, the chapter presents some reflection on the policy implications of these issues and some suggestions for future research.

ECONOMIC DEVELOPMENT IN MICHIGAN

The lessons from the examination of economic development practices among Michigan cities in Chapter 3 appear straightforward. Overall, Michigan cities rely heavily on traditional supply-side strategies to foster economic development. The main thrust of policy efforts appears to be attracting capital from other areas to foster continued local industrial development.

State enabling legislation provides broad discretion to cities in choosing economic development techniques. Statutes regulating financial incentives such as tax abatements, bond sales, and loan arrangements are particularly liberal. Indeed, a comparison with national data suggests that Michigan cities tend to rely more heavily on standard financial incentives than most other states. Analysis of data from the 1989 economic development survey conducted by the International City/County Management Association indicates that, nationally, only moderate percentages of cities use financial incentives. For example, 35% use tax abatements, 83% provide for deferred tax payments, 17% offer loan guarantees, 22% grant loan subsidies, 2% offer direct loans, and 37% issue bonds for private development. As noted in Chapter 3, the rates for Michigan cities are much higher; 83% use tax abatements, 24% offer loan guarantees, 28% allow loan subsidies, 28% provide direct loans, and 39% issue bonds. Only the use of deferred tax payments (11%) is lower among Michigan cities.

It is apparent that Michigan cities are more likely to utilize financial techniques than either Ontario cities or other U.S. cities, particularly in the use of tax abatements. This no doubt reflects a variety of factors, including past trends in development policy, regional geographic location, the manufacturing base of the economy, and the extent of economic stress. But, the ability of cities to engage in such practices under state law also has a significant impact on what strategies cities employ.

Since competition plays a significant role in shaping the economic development practices of individual cities, the use of tax abatements in Michigan has a growth dynamic of its own. When cities in the state use financial incentives to attract industry, this encourages others to do the same and increases the use of such mechanisms. And, as the explanatory models show, cities which are particularly distressed are more likely to offer all the incentives available to stay in the game. To use the earlier metaphor, they are shooting at everything.

ECONOMIC DEVELOPMENT IN ONTARIO

The analysis in Chapter 4 described a somewhat different situation in Ontario, although the differences tend to be of scale rather than content.

Cities in Ontario generally use the same types of economic development techniques to the same extent as cities in Michigan. However, provincial enabling legislation differs in one important respect--cities in Ontario are prohibited from offering financial "bonuses" such as tax incentives, loan arrangements, and bond sales. As a result, cities in Ontario seldom use such incentives. Such practices are not absent, however, as noted earlier. In responding to the survey, a small number of city officials indicated that they used such incentives, and in face-to-face interviews officials frequently indicated that other cities in the province employed such mechanisms. As a general rule, however, the limitation on financial incentives appears to push cities to use more demand-side approaches toward economic development. Thus, cities in Ontario are more likely to engage in worker training programs, research and development initiatives, export market development, and the like.

The affects of this enabling legislation on competition between cities is somewhat mixed. Local officials in Ontario indicated repeatedly in face-to-face interviews that provincial restrictions on financial incentives reduced at least the perception of competition between cities. However, survey questions about intercity competition indicated high levels of perceived competition both with other cities in the province and across the U.S./Canadian border. Competition within the province tended to occur at the provincial legislature, however, as cities jockeyed to win approval for special provincial tax abatements or other financial incentives.

POLICY CONVERGENCE

The findings in Chapter 5 seem to support a growing academic literature which suggests that local economic development policy is converging between the U.S. and Canada. Local economic development policies appear to be driven by the same forces in cities throughout the post-industrial world; international business fluctuations, competition between nations for development, and transportation and communication advances allowing for separation of production and management functions and markets. Differences, when they exist, reflect a different social legacy, national agenda, or governmental and legislative framework. While Ontario and Michigan cities differ somewhat in local government structure and the organization of economic development, governing arrangements are similar. The key actors and the locus of control are the same. Problem definition, as reflected by goals, is also quite uniform. Thus, economic development policy, driven as it is by common international economic forces, is more similar than different, with the variation largely a function of different statutory environments.

ECONOMIC DEVELOPMENT PROFESSIONALS

One of the main arguments developed here is that explanations of local economic development policy-making have been limited by inattention to the role and environment of professionals. While there is a large literature arguing that local economic development policy is strongly affected by international economic forces, the analysis here has stressed that local officials can have an independent affect on policy even given these broader economic constraints. Local officials may not be able to control whether their region is experiencing economic growth or decline. They may not be able to do much about industrial shifts and the concomitant population relocation. But, they can affect how the city reacts to these forces. To refer to an earlier analogy, they serve as midwives in producing economic development for the community.

City officials employ many strategies to cope with economic stress: efforts to reduce governmental budgets and the public workforce, to be more productive with current resources, to privatize and/or contract out services, to shed responsibilities, to increase taxes or impose service fees, to implement intergovernmental agreements, to employ various debt strategies, or simply do nothing in hopes of riding out the situation. Beyond these general strategies, the package of economic development techniques chosen by a community is affected by local decisions. Given this, it becomes vital to understand which local officials are making the policy-decisions and on what basis those decisions are being made.

The analysis here does not suggest that economic development professionals make such decisions alone, to the exclusion of elected officials or even citizen or business leaders. As one economic development professional suggested, "ultimately we don't make the decisions--the job of the professional is to be as square with the elected officials as possible." It does argue, however, that they have an important role which has been largely overlooked in the academic literature. Some economic development activities are clearly major or "pivotal" events. Large sections of a city are razed, people relocated, land purchased, and infrastructure developed for a new industrial site. These are the kinds of economic development activities which make news. To use the language of Jones and Bachelor (1993), they are "peak events." Hence they are clearly within the purview of elected officials, often the chief executive. They are intensely and visibly political in that there are clear winners and losers. The public takes sides, courts are often involved, and usually such projects involve multiple levels of government and complex funding arrangements. An elected chief executive typically is needed to serve as the visible figurehead for such efforts.

However, most of what occurs in economic development on a day-to-day basis does not involve such events. Survey responses, interviews with professionals, anecdotal evidence, and previous research all point to the fact that much local economic development activity is, in fact, routine. Further, these routine decisions--preparing and using promotional materials, visiting existing or potential firms, operating a downtown development authority, participating in a trade show--are largely controlled and implemented by economic development professionals. And, to the extent that professionals use their knowledge and expertise to shape the debate and delineate the options examined by elected officials, they have a major role in decisions about "peak events" as well.

148

Thus, the literature on bureaucratic professionals in other areas of urban governance becomes pertinent. To summarize: since environments are stressful and uncertain; since professionals must answer to political leaders and the citizenry for their jobs; since they face multiple stakeholders with numerous and often conflicting demands; since there is competition between cities; and, most important, since so much about what constitutes economic development is not well understood even by the professionals themselves, decision rules or simplifying procedures become a necessary fact of life. The task of "economic development" is defined by a particular solution set which frames the problems and the options available. The fact that economic development officials tend to "throw spaghetti at the wall" says little about their professional training or what they would do in optimal circumstances. Rather, it speaks volumes about the situational environment in which they find themselves.

In fact, when it comes to the use of decision rules or solution sets, the actions of elected and appointed officials converge. The literature has highlighted the operative role of each of these actors in local governing regimes. The regime, typically initiated by elected officials and comprised primarily of business or other "resourced" interests (at least for corporate regimes), identifies problems, generates solutions, and assembles the resources to implement necessary social production functions. According to Jones and Bachelor (1993), each regime conducts this process within the confines of "solution sets," that is, systems of problem definition and preferred solutions developed and employed by the regime in the past and changed only incrementally over time. Thus, in the collective memory and consciousness of regime members, economic development goals become defined in predictable ways with fairly uniform techniques or strategies utilized. Such solution sets regularize patterns of interaction among regime participants and reduce the need for constant control of the process by elites.

At the same time, to the extent that decision-making is left to professionals, again, largely the case for routine matters, these forces are compounded. When the regime is functioning as it should, and conflict over development issues is controlled, elected officials are even more prone to leave decisions to the "advice of experts" (Baumgartner, 1989). Standard operating procedures and professionally-based criteria, or even throwing spaghetti, take over as criteria for decision-making. These, too, are heavily influenced by past efforts and the actions of other communities. In this way the solution sets employed by regimes and the decision-rules used by economic development professionals have compounding and mutually reinforcing effects.

POLITICS, ECONOMICS, OR BUREAUCRATIC ROUTINES?

The final focus of the analysis was the development of a comprehensive model depicting both how economic development policies are made and how such decision-making processes affect the ultimate policies implemented. In short, the goal was to examine the relative effects of economic forces, governmental structure, competition for economic development among cities, resources devoted to development, locus of control, and the decision-making procedures employed, specifically rational planning as opposed to goal displacement and shooting behaviors. Chapters 7 and 8 offered several lessons on these issues.

The analysis indicates that both economic forces and local decisions influence local economic development policy-making. However, their relative impacts appear to be contextual. The presence of severe economic stress appears determinative. If a community is experiencing high unemployment and low levels of growth and residents are poor, then there is little economic development officials can do but throw spaghetti at the wall. Fiscal stress and competition from other cities appear to limit the opportunities for rational decision-making and stimulate officials to employ any and all techniques in hopes that something will work. Thus, planning is a luxury to be ignored in the face of political demands for jobs on the part of residents, tax base on the part of elected officials, and inducements on the part of the business community. In short, a buyers' market prevails and there is little that can be done to foster long-range planning. Indeed, there is no long range or rational planning in the sense of identification of goals, exploration of alternatives, analysis of likely outcomes, and evaluation of actions taken. However, it should be recognized that goal displacement and shooting behaviors are a rational response to uncertainty, stress, and competition in the environment.

Absent such pressures, there are things a local community can do to foster rational planning and evaluation. Increased resources devoted to economic development and efforts to professionalize the economic development function appear to produce more rational and/or goal directed behavior on the part of development officials. As noted in Chapter 7, this is the classic "good news/bad news" story. The good news is that under conditions of fiscal health, or at least limited economic stress, local officials can take actions which serve to rationalize economic development efforts, utilizing more goal directed efforts and targeting the needs of the community. The bad news is that under conditions of extreme economic stress, economic development professionals are going to shoot at everything that flies, and little can be done to limit this behavior.

The relationship between economic stress and local control can be likened to a box. The regional, state, national, and even international economies operate to determine the environment for local economic development decision-making; in other words, they define the size of the box. Some cities operate in a very large box; a favorable economic environment provides many options, much discretion, and more resources for local officials. For these cities, growth management strategies, linkage policies, performance requirements, and the like are all possible. Other cities, however, are constrained by a very small box and local options become more limited. This reality was summarized by one economic development official in Michigan; "If we were in a crisis situation we would be less selective. We aren't going to take anyone that comes down the road. Because we have low unemployment (2.8%) we don't have to rely on the market for what it gives us. We're not in the job-buying business here." An official in a growing Ontario city made a similar statement indicating that "the city will counsel away any business that doesn't seem to fit here or where this is not the best place." This is the luxury of operating in a bigger box.

What difference this all makes in a policy sense is not clear at this point. The economic development outcomes, the particular policy packages chosen by communities, are not explained very well by the models presented here. Economic factors, competition, governmental structure, resources, and the decision-patterns of officials only partially explain the actual policies employed in a community. Obviously, this is the continuing challenge to both academic analysts and practitioners.

THE FUTURE OF CROSS-NATIONAL COMPARISONS

In its totality, the analysis presented here strongly supports the contention that comparing local economic development efforts by cities in Canada and the U.S. is valid and instructive. Clearly, more work needs to be done both in cross-national comparison and in the development of explanatory decision-making theory. Thus, as in many intellectual pursuits, the main contribution here may be in identifying questions which remained unanswered.

1) Are Canadian and U.S. cities converging in other areas of local policy, or is the economic development policy arena unique because of international economic forces?

2) Are Michigan and Ontario cities sufficiently representative to conclude a theory of convergence? Clearly the premise of the book and the analysis presented argue that they are. However, comparison of national data sets may be necessary to confirm this initial finding.

3) Exactly how do routine and pivotal events interact in economic development and how does the locus of control shift from elected to appointed actors? Research is clearly needed to more explicitly examine the interrelationships between elected and appointed officials, either through the development of data bases which contain responses from a significant number and variety of policy actors or through numerous and intensive comparative case studies.

4) What important explanatory factors are still missing from the analysis? More thought needs to be given to other variables which can extend current models of development policy-making. What variables might better explain differences in the policies employed by cities? Such factors might include the actions or decisions of business leaders or citizens; more refined measures of the resources, budgetary and otherwise, devoted to economic development; accurate measures of policy emulation or diffusion; and more sensitive measures of economic stress and changes in the composition of the economic base. This list is suggestive; there are undoubtedly others.

SOME POLICY IMPLICATIONS

The analysis here also raises some interesting policy issues for future consideration. Specifically, the decision-making models appear to support a greater commitment of resources to economic development activities. The findings may be of interest to many economic development professionals, perhaps providing a rationale for budget presentations before city councils.

It appears that increased resources and a more professionalized economic development function mitigate stress and uncertainty in the environment and thus reduce dysfunctional behaviors such as goal displacement and shooting. Unless a community is severely distressed, it seems clear that rational planning and goal-directed behavior can be promoted through increased support and training for economic development professionals. Further, Chapter 8 suggested that greater resources will lead to more entrepreneurial marketing activities along with land and site management and acquisition activities.

Even given this, however, a fundamental question remains; what difference does this make for the success of economic development efforts? While more resources and professionalism may lead to more rational activity, are the resultant economic development policies more successful at generating economic development? This, of course, is a critical question directing the course of future research. To answer it, practitioners and academics must settle on a definition of success in local economic development. There has been little attention to this thus far. Clearly the goal for future research is the development of a cross-national theory which explains why cities do what they do, but also assesses what works, and what exactly that means.

REFERENCES

Baumgartner, F.R. 1989. Strategies of political leadership in diverse settings. In B.D. Jones (ed.), *Leadership and politics* (114-134). Lawrence, Kansas: University Press of Kansas.

Jones, B.D. and Bachelor, L.W. 1986,1993. *The sustaining hand.* Lawrence, Kansas: University Press of Kansas.

Regression Analysis
Hypothesized Model

	b	Beta	Significance
Rationality $r^2=.06$			
shooting	.15	-.18	.09
goal displacement	-.19	.15	.17
Shooting $r^2=.02$			
goal displacement	-.01	-.01	.91
rationality	.15	.15	.17
Goal Displacement $r^2=.25$			
turbulence	.51	.50	.00
bureaucrats	.07	.07	.41
Bureaucrats $r^2=.00$			
professionalism	-.01	-.01	.92
resources	.01	.01	.92
Turbulence $r^2=.19$			
professionalism	-.07	-.07	.56
resources	-.40	-.43	.00
Resources $r^2=.22$			
health	.36	.37	.00
reformism	.17	.16	.13
mayor	-.02	-.01	.94
competition	.15	.15	.17
Professionalism $r^2=.16$			
competition	.07	.07	.54
reformism	.13	.13	.27
mayor	-.77	-.38	.00
health	.09	.08	.50

APPENDIX **B**
**Survey Classification of
Economic Development Mechanisms**

Marketing Activities
Business liaison committees
Inventory of available sites
Brochure sent to prospects
Videos sent to prospects
Visits to prospects
Soliciting foreign business
Trade shows
Developing export markets
Promoting specific sites
Market development planning

Governance Tools and Infrastructure
Improved/expanded parking
Improved traffic circulation/streets
Improved street cleaning, garbage collection services
Improved pedestrian amenities (plantings, benches)
Aesthetic improvements
Improved/expanded recreation facilities
Incentives for historic preservation
Improved/created sewage collection/treatment systems
Improved/created water treatment/distribution systems
Creating community improvement areas

Governmental Regulations
Consolidated/one-stop permit issuance
Improved building inspection system or process
Ombudsperson to help resolve problems
Height and density variances
Density transfers
Modified zoning process
Relaxed environmental regulations or procedure
Adopted historic district regulation
Adopted sign control regulations
Adopted facade control regulations
Adopted anti-litter regulations/programs
Industrial zoning
Design requirements for industrial parks

Land and Property Management Activities
Lot consolidation
Land expropriation
Land acquisition
Business relocation
Clearing land
Sale of land to developers
Leasing of land to developers
Office/retail property management
Rehabilitation of old buildings
City-owned industrial parks
Enterprise zones

Financial Tools
Tax abatements
Deferred tax payments
Loan guarantees
Loan subsidies
Direct loans
Sale lease-back arrangements
In-kind services
Donations of unused real property
Awards/funding for research initiatives
Business incubators
Employee training/retraining
Provisions for assisted housing
Awards for private industry achievement

INDEX

159